DANISH YEARBOOK
OF
PHILOSOPHY

VOLUME 27

DANISH YEARBOOK
OF
PHILOSOPHY

VOLUME 27

1992

MUSEUM TUSCULANUM PRESS
UNIVERSITY OF COPENHAGEN 1992

published for
The Society for Philosophy and Psychology, Copenhagen,
in cooperation with
the Philosophical Societies of Aarhus and Odense
and with financial support from
the Danish Research Council for the Humanities

*

*

Articles for consideration and all editorial communications should be sent in five copies to:
Danish Yearbook of Philosophy
University of Copenhagen, Department of Philosophy
Njalsgade 80, DK 2300 Copenhagen S, Denmark

Business communications, including subscriptions and orders for reprints, should be addressed to the publishers:
MUSEUM TUSCULANUM PRESS
Njalsgade 94
DK 2300 Copenhagen S
Denmark

*

PRINTED IN DENMARK
BY SPECIAL-TRYKKERIET VIBORG

ISBN 87-7289-193-9
ISSN 0070-2749

CONTENTS

Danish Yearbook of Philosophy, Vol. **27** (1992), 7-22

HEIDEGGER'S CONCEPT OF TRUTH: SEMANTICS AND RELATIVISM

Nils Holtug
University of Copenhagen

> Vorausgesetzt, dass die Wahrheit
> ein Weib ist
> *Nietzsche*

The concept of truth seems to be one of the most puzzling in philosophy, not only because it is, in itself, problematic to give an account of it, but also because our qualification of this concept has implications for a number of other concepts, such as realism/idealism/anti-realism, reference and meaning. Thus, it is unclear exactly what relations connect truth, reference and meaning. According to some philosophers, understanding a sentence is constituted by the semantic agents knowledge of the truth conditions,[1] whereas others claim that truth, meaning and reference are, essentially, mutually independent concepts.[2] How we work out the concept of truth, again, depends how much explanatory power we wish to assign to it. Amongst the vast amount of suggestions that have surfaced by now, we might mention the correspondence theory (in different versions), the redundancy theory, the coherence theory and the pragmatic theory of truth.

In the following we shall advance an interpretation of Heidegger's concept of truth, according to which truth is closely connected to meaning, and Heidegger, in his theory of knowledge, commits himself to a relativistic position. As we shall see, these two points are related. Now, relativism is a somewhat strained concept, both regarding exactly what it is thought to capture, and whether it is consistent. But to clarify the first aspect, we shall specify relativism as a commitment to the following two propositions:

(A) Different conceptual horizons can hold incompatible theories/beliefs.
(B) There are no objective criteria, that can privilege one theory/belief, held within one conceptual horizon, above another, incompatible, theory/belief, held within another conceptual horizon.

However, (A) and (B) still need clarification in four respects. Firstly, by "incompatible theories/beliefs" we mean the same theories/beliefs ascribed different truth-values, thus p and non-p will be incompatible.[3] Secondly, the horizons in (A) and (B) are determined spatio-temporally, that is, both by specific periods in time and geographically (in the former case we have a relativistic version of the thesis of historicity, in the latter, we have cultural relativism). So this kind of relativism doesn't pertain at an individual level, but only between horizons of linguistic communities.[4] Thirdly, what we are discussing is epistemic, not ontological, relativism, even though it might be claimed that this distinction isn't coherent. According to epistemic relativism the world is explained in different ways within different horizons (that in some sense have equal worth), but this is not necessarily to claim that there is no specific way, in which the world (an-sich) is. However, on this ontological question, we shall be agnostic. Fourthly, what (B) denies is not merely the existence of a unique privileged framework from which to assess incorrigible knowledge-claims (this is denied by almost all post-positivists), but furthermore the objectivity (in any potent sense of the word) of our critical assessment of competing criteria of justification. Thus, *whenever* two competing conceptual horizons employ different criteria of justification for some proposition p, it is possible that, even in ideal conditions, no amount of rational debat will settle the issue of which criteria are those relevant for assessing p. This, combined with (A), gives us a substantial version of relativism.

Our thesis is neither that Heidegger's being a relativist provides us with a reductio argument against him, nor that relativism is a theory we ought to embrace, but merely *that* he is a relativist; in other words, whether Heidegger's relativism is to be considered a strength or a weakness is left to the reader's own philosophical judgement. Also, as a last introductory remark, we shall be giving some subsidiary arguments along the way, which are not to be found in Heidegger's own text, but this is necessary because Heidegger doesn't systematically address the problem of relativism. However, it must be legitimate to try to focus the attention on the main claims of a philosophical position, and see what follows or is reasonably implied, in order to be able to evaluate the soundness of that position.

I

In *Sein und Zeit* (SuZ) the analysis of truth (§ 44) starts off by characterizing the traditional concept of truth, and its limits. This traditional concept, has been predominant from Aristotle to Kant (and in modern philosophy of language, we might, amongst others, include the early Wittgenstein). Its central claims are: (a) the "locus" of truth is the proposition (judgement), and (b) the essence of truth is in the "agreement" of the judgement with its object.[5] However, the question is what is meant by "agreement", and why propositions have this status. Agreement is a relation between two (or more) objects, where the identity-relation (x=y) is the special case where the two coincide. In the traditional concept of truth this has typically been construed as an agreement of "intellectus" and "res", or subject and object. In the correspondence theory, in philosophy of language, a true proposition has to correspond (somehow) to an external reality. Both these concepts have subjective and objective versions, according to which the intellect/proposition has to "agree" with, respectively, sense-data and an object "an-sich". But how can we imagine such agreement possible, can we legitimately ascribe the same kind of Being (Sein) to the participating elements? This question presupposes that we know what is meant by "Being", and so we must be permitted a digression to Heidegger's concept of intentionality.

"Dasein" is intentionaly directed at an entity (Seiende). The condition of possibility of this directedness is "Dasein"s being open[6] (Erschlossen) to meaning (Sinn,[7] intentionalen Richtungs-sinn[8]), that is, "Dasein"'s being open to the concepts by which it can interpret entities, that is, "Dasein"'s being able to use the concepts by which it can interpret entities. Alternatively, we can put this as ""Dasein"'s openness to Being". This is because "Dasein" in its facticity (Fakticität) / thrownness (Geworfenheit) is within a specific horizon of meaning, a leeway of significance, that permits it to project itself understandingly on entities, that is, interpret entities in their Being = interpret them within the relevant leeway of concepts.[9] All according to which type of entity "Dasein" interprets, it will be thrown on/limited to a specific frame of concepts, within which it, in a meaningful way, will be able to refer to the entity. Indeed, Heidegger distinguishes between different kinds of Being, namely "Vorhanden*sein*", "Zuhanden*sein*" and "Eksistenz". These are the "areas" of regional ontology (semantics). Now, even a simpel predication, "x is P", presupposes openness to Being, that is, openness to the predicate P, to *is* (which can be used in different senses, ie. Vx, Px, x=y). An openness, that is the condition of possibility of identifying x in the first place.[10]

Admittedly, this is a somewhat controversial interpretation of "Being". However, I think it has a number of advantages, including the following: (a) it enables us to account for some of the standard problems facing Heidegger scholars, such as *why* Being is presupposed in any interpretation (Auslegung), and *how* Heidegger can claim that "Dasein" is not a substance, essentially characterized by reflexive conciousness (as in Husserl), (b) it says something plausible, (c) it permits us to maintain the concept of "ontological difference" (because, on the ontological level, meaning is not an entity, but what is always *presupposed* in any inquiry into entities), and (d) it doesn't make Being into an essence or quasi-essence, as most other interpretations (that is, those that don't just remain silent about how we are to understand "Being").

By now we can introduce Heidegger's criticism of the traditional concept of truth. Truth is not a relation of correspondence between a subject and an object, or generally, between two entities present-at-hand (Vorhandenes), because "Dasein"'s access to entities primarily doesn't come under this Being (Vorhandensein).[11] "Dasein"'s primary access is in the use of the entity (in which case it is ready-to-hand (Zuhanden)), and furthermore, the ready-to-hand is claimed to be the condition of possibility of the present-to-hand. In other words, a proposition (the "Apophantische Als") presupposes usage (the "Hermeneutische Als"), and thus the correspondence theory reflects a departure from original intentionality. However, it is not only in this respect the traditional concept of truth turns out to be limited, we also have to be *open* to relations (aRb, a=b), or generally, a horizon of meaning, to interpret entities. This, again, means that we have no access to a concept-independent reality, that could verify our propositions. Now, the question is whether Heidegger, ultimately, can forward his concept of truth without acknowledging some sort of "agreement" as constitutive. But, Heidegger's criticism seems more directed at how restricted the traditional concept is, than demanding a fundamental dismissal of the correspondence theory.

II

How, then, are we to understand truth? Heidegger initially gives the following two characterizations: "Die Aussage ist wahr, bedeutet: sie entdeckt das Seiende an ihm selbst",[12] and "...Wahrheit im ursprünglichsten Sinne ist die Erschlossenheit des Daseins...".[13] Now, it would seem natural to conclude: truth=("Dasein"'s) openness (Erschlossenheit)=uncovering (Entdeckung). However, this would neglect the twofold structure (ambiguity) of the truth-concept in Heidegger. Heidegger is primarily interested in the *condition of possibility* of truth (and in being so, he radicalizes the phenomenological project). How come, a proposition (as a special instance of "Entdeckung", "Sein-bei" or "Intentionalität") has truth conditions at all? This is only possible because "Dasein"'s Being essentially is openness. "Dasein" has a fore-conception (Vorgriff) of the Being of entities, that is, an understanding of the conceptual horizon within which entities can be interpreted, and this is the condition of possibility of both "Der vorprädikative Character der Als-Struktur"[14] and predication, "x *is* P". Accordingly, the concept of truth has the following twofold structure:

(1) "Dasein"'s openness.
(2) Specific truth (the uncovering (Entdeckung) of entities within-the-world (Innerweltliches Seiendes)).

Furthermore, (1) is the condition of possibility of (2), or, as Heidegger puts it, the traditional concept of truth is "derived" from the primordial phenomenon of truth (ursprüngliche Phänomen der Wahrheit) ((1)).[15] The truth of propositions (specific truth) is limited by, but simultaneously possible because of, "Dasein"'s facticity, that is, the leeway of meaning at its disposal, or, in other words, only because "Dasein" is in the world (In-der-Welt-sein), specific truth is possible. However, Heidegger doesn't make it clear exactly what the argument is, but as far as I can see we can give (at least) three justifying reasons: (a) formulating a proposition presupposes a conceptual horizon, (b) identifying an entity, as being this or that, presupposes a conceptual horizon, and (c) agreement/identity presupposes a conceptual horizon, in which it is possible for entities to participate in these relations.

Having isolated the two aspects of truth, we can treat them separately. Heidegger characterizes "Dasein"'s openness as constituted by thrownness

(Geworfenheit), projection (Entwurf) and falling (Verfallen).[16] But what does he mean by this new truth-constituent, "falling"?[17] In so far "Dasein" is open (Erschlossen), it is also closed (Verschlossen), and in so far "Dasein" is "in the truth", it is also "in the untruth".[18] The point is not that in so far "Dasein" says something true, it also says something false, this would be inconsistent. "Dasein"'s openness to a horizon of meaning makes it possible for a proposition to have truth-conditions, but not to ascribe truth and falsehood simultaneously. But in so far "Dasein", in its openness, uncovers entities true or falsely, it simultaneously closes of other possible meanings. In this sense, every uncovering presupposes both openness and closedness. The implication is that even when "Dasein" carries out an uncovering that is true, there will be competing alternatives, within other conceptual horizons (maybe even within the very same). The question is how radically this point is to be taken, is it possible that a true proposition, within one conceptual horizon, is false within another horizon? Initially this seems possible, given Heidegger characterization of simultaneous openness and closedness, but later we shall discuss whether Heidegger can avoid this consequence. However, before we are able to engage in an adequate discussion, we will have to account for the other aspect of truth, specific truth.

Heidegger doesn't say too much about truth-criteria in *SuZ*, and we shall, in accordance with Tugendhat, characterize this as a neglection.[19] Remember, that "Dasein" primarily meets entities in the context of use, as ready-to-hand (Zuhanden). Now, Heidegger claims that when we in a proposition uncover an entity, "so, wie es an ihm selbst ist",[20] we are presupposing the category ready-to-handness (Zuhandenheit).[21] We won't discuss this ontological privilege of ready-to-handness above present-to-handness (Vorhandenheit), but shall merely be presupposing it in the following. Now, the criterion of the truth of a proposition, is that the meaning actually uncovers the entity, of which it speaks. What is to count for the meaning actually uncovering the entity, is determined by opennes (truth in the sense of (1)), and so we might say that this is the formal, or second order, criterion. That a proposition is true if the meaning uncovers the entity in question, is of course somewhat commonplace, and the question is how we are able to ascertain whether the uncovering actually takes place. Here, the teleological structure of entities seems to be important to Heidegger. If we take a proposition about an item of equipment (Zeug), "the vacuum cleaner is effective", a test of this claim, that is, you turn it on to find out whether it actually cleans in accordance with what you would have to expect from a vacuum cleaner, that was to live up to the predicate "effective", will determine the truth-value of the proposition. In this account, we have had to include the concept of "agreement" in some sense (although we could have characterized the relationship between the entity, as it is *meant* in the proposition, and as it intrinsically is, as one of identity). Thus, the criterion of the truth of a proposition, is that what in the proposition is *meant* about an entity, is such, as the entity would appear in a possible *verifying intentionality*. What is claimed is essentially that:

(T) "p" is true, if and only if, p
and
p, if and only if, p can be verified.

The first part of (T) amounts to a minimalistic theory of truth, in accordance with Tarski's, the second part seems to commit Heidegger to anti-realism or verificationism. If we interpret Heidegger as a verificationist, he denies that we can, in a meaningful way, interpret an entity if we don't have criteria of verification. This is, as far as I can see, a plausible interpretation, because if (i) it is only meaningful to talk of an uncovering in so far we can verify that one has taken place, and (ii) understanding is of the meaning assigned in the uncovering, then we only have understanding in so far we have criteria of verification.[22]

A strength in this interpretation of Heidegger as a verificationist or anti-realist, that is, as denying the existence of verification-transcendent truths,[23] is furthermore that this enables us to account for why he says that "Bevor die Gesetze Newtons entdeckt wurden, waren sie nicht »wahr«".[24]

As we have seen, the first part of (T) only amounts to a minimalistic theory of truth, something any theory of truth must be able to account for, and it doesn't commit us to a stronger sort of correspondence theory. For instance, Davidson unites it with the coherence theory of truth.[25] The second part doesn't determine the matter either, because it isn't clear exactly what it means to verify p. Again, amongst others, the (stronger) correspondence theory, the coherence theory, and the pragmatic theory seem to be possible candidates.[26] This, I think, in itself gives us a reason not to make Heidegger into an adherent of the strong correspondence theory, because then he would have to face all the traditional problems; accounting for a language-independent reality, for what exactly "correspondence" means, counterfactuals etc. (and as we have seen, some of these problems actually make him distance himself from a traditional correspondence theory).

In other words, we have to agree with Tugendhat, when he claims that the concept of specific truth is neglected by Heidegger, the specific criteria are not specified. However, Günter Figal has recently claimed, against Tugendhat, that it is possible to maintain a concept of specific truth in Heidegger. First of all, "Entdecken" is not identical to the proposition, because what is to be uncovered has to be uncoverable already,[27] as we have seen. "Entdecken" is not itself a phenomenon we can uncover, since phenomena are, exactly, what shows itself (sich zeigen) in the uncovering. "Entdecken" (specified as the uncovering inherent in the use of equipement) is the condition of possibility of propositional truth/falsehood, and hence not something we can uncover as an entity. And it is this primary, pre-predicative meaning of "Entdecken", that is covered up (verdecken) in discourse (the proposition). Thus the covering up, in the proposition, doesn't refer to anything false/wrong being communicated, it can be perfectly true, "...wobei es dann eine Frage von sekundärer Bedeutung ist, nach welchem Kriterien man diese Wahrheit beurteilt".[28] However, if you want to have a concept of truth at all, it seems to me that you have to say something about these criteria, in other words, I'm in accordance with Tugendhat when he says "Dass ein Wahrheitsbegriff auf die Aussagewahrheit passt, ist eine minimalbedingung, die er erfüllen muss, wenn er überhaupt ein Wahrheitsbegriff sein soll".[29]

III

Given Heidegger's account of truth being relative to "Dasein", does a more traditional concept of relativism follow?[30] As we have already seen, Heidegger seems to acknowledge the possibility of different assignments of truth-values to a given proposition, within different horizons of meaning. However, there are a number of different theories, that might allow him to avoid relativism (as defined above), namely (i) there is only one possible adequate uncovering of an entity, since there is only one adequate horizon of meaning, (ii) if different horizons of meaning assign different truth-values to a specific proposition, they are really not talking about the same proposition at all, (iii) we can only understand another horizon of meaning if we presuppose the truth of most their sentences (beliefs), and hence we shall never encounter anyone whose propositions we, predominantly, assign different truth-values to, and (iv) "Dasein"'s Being is universal, and sets certain limitations to which uncoverings are possible (I don't imagine I have supplied an exhaustive list). The problem with (i)-(iii) is that they are quite possibly objections to relativism, but there is no mention of them in *SuZ*. Still, if we interpret Heidegger as an anti-realist, (ii) seems to be just what we are looking for. But then again, I'm uncertain about (ii) because it seems to me that it shows too much. The point is that if, within two horizons of meaning, there are different procedures of justification/proof connected to a specific proposition p, p doesn't have the same meaning within these horizons. So how identify p, given this asymmetry? However, this seems to be a problem for any anti-realist. Let "Goldbach's conjecture" be a yet unproven conjecture of mathematics. The anti-realist will now claim that understanding the conjecture consists in a (publicly accessible) understanding of what has to be the case for it to be true, that is, the procedures of justification/proof. But these procedures are not accessible. Given this situation, how are we able to identify the theorem the day the proof is available, with what we have hitherto called "Goldbach's conjecture". The point is that the problem of identification is not only a problem for the anti-realist relativist, but for any anti-realism with a claim to plausibility (but, of course, this argument will mean nothing to someone who isn't inclined towards anti-realism).

Still, there exists an anti-realist answer to the problem, that might show how identification is possible without undermining (ii). Neil Tennant argues that according to anti-realist semantics, the grasp of the meaning of a sentence (in this case, Goldbach's conjecture) consists in an ability to decide whether or not a particular representation establishes the truth (proof) of the sentence (and this is quite close to Dummett's formulation).[31] Hence there is no problem in identifying Goldbach's conjecture, because the meaning of it is constituted, both before and after the discovery of the proof, by the proof. However, this solution seems to be problematic within an anti-realist framework. This is because, before the discovery of the proof, we will never be able to know whether anyone understands the conjecture, since we can't present them with the proof and see if they are willing to acknowledge it as such, and therefore, on this construal of meaning, either the conjecture has no (definite) meaning, or, contrary to the Wittgensteinian insight, use falls short of establishing meaning (indeed, whether anyone understands the conjecture, is, at least temporarily (until the proof is found), verification-transcendent).

So, as Dummett suggests elsewhere,[32] maybe it is sufficient to have a *generel* knowledge of rules of inference, correct transition and so on, to be able to grasp the meaning of a yet unproven sentence. In this sense we could know what we would be willing to accept as a proof of a particular sentence. However, it is quite unclear how this generel knowledge could individuate the sentence, that is, determine its meaning uniquely and distinct from from all those other sentences that would need to apply the same generel rules for their proof. It is no use claiming, at this point, that the rules wouldn't be applied in exactly the same order and involve exactly the same axioms, because which order and which axioms would have to be known in advance, for a unique pre-proof identification of the sentence.

Where did all this take us? (ii) was meant to provide an argument to refute relativism by claiming that sentences, which have different procedures of justification, will differ in meaning, and thus there is no possibility of disagreement on this account. But what we have seen is that anti-realism, in virtue of which Heidegger might be thought to be able to use (ii) as an argument, is actually ill advised to connect meaning-identity and justification as close as (ii) requires. This will make identification of the sort discussed (Goldbach's conjecture before and after proof) impossible. Of course, it might be the case that the problem can't be solved, and this would indeed put both Heidegger and anti-realism generally in grave difficulties. But it is worth noting that relativism, qua relativism, doesn't put the anti-realist in trouble as grave as this (and relativism is the main focus of the discussion here). As Crispin Wright points out, criteria (of justification) are always defeasible.[33] This means that if, say, Crispin ascribes a mental property, e.g. having a headache, to Michael, upon Michaels exposing criterial headache-behaviour (moaning, holding his head, complaining about the pain in his forehead), it is always possible that even though these criteria are satisfied, further evidence can show that the claim to Michaels having a headache isn't warranted (Michael might be simulating). If Crispin finds out that Michael was simulating, we (and he) will want to say that he was previously wrong, when he said that Michael had a headache. But this is only possible if the meaning of the sentence "Michael has a headache" hasn't changed after the original criterial ground has been defeated.

What this shows is that, once again, the anti-realist should be careful not to tie meaning-synonymy *too* intimately to criteria/justification. It might be objected that all the example shows is that Michaels not simulating was part of the original criteria of which Crispin should have been aware, but this would be to miss the point that "Michael is simulating", in any behavioural manifestation, is also defeasible (indeed, a criterion might be defeated often enough to prevent us from ever ascribing headaches on this basis). So meaning-synonymy must be possible even though there is (at least) a minimal variation in the criteria of justification. And this is all the relativist needs; if Crispin and Martin agree on everything that would, respectively, be taken/ not taken to warrant the assertion that Michael has a headache, they could still disagree on how to weigh the different (multiple) criteria (Crispin is primarily impressed by the painful expression on Michaels face, Martin by the fact that Michael is acting in a play), and thus ascribe different truth-values to the assertion. According to Crispin Wright, the fact that they agree on what does/doesn't warrant the assertion, is enough to ensure that the assertion to which they attach different truth-values is the same.[34] If, however, the fact that they weigh the criteria differently is judged sufficient for claiming that they are actually employing different criteria, we must remind the reader that different weighing of criteria is a minimal variation in criteria (if at all), and as we have already pointed out, this must be possible without loosing the identity of the sentences. So, on an anti-realist theory (maybe more the anti-realism of Crispin Wright than that of Dummett), (ii) does not provide an argument against relativism.

(iii) is Davidson's argument.[35] However, it seems to me that Davidson's restrictions on interpretation are too strong. Though I cannot argue this at any length here, it seems to me that, even if we accept Davidson's premise that we initially have to presuppose the truth of beliefs within another horizon of meaning when interpreting them (the principle of charity), this doesn't supply any *apriori* evidence that we won't be able to make so many modifications (in the beliefs we attribute) along the way, that we actually end up with predominantly conflicting sets of beliefs between us and the people interpreted. Thus, the restrictions need to be loosened, and Davidson's argument on interpretation doesn't pull through.[36] (iv), that is, the claim that "Dasein"'s Being is universal, and sets certain limitations to which uncoverings are possible, seems to be a possible interpretation of Heidegger. Gethmann points out, in accordance with this interpretation, that the problem of relativism in Heidegger pertains only to the truth of propositions and not to primordial truth, because primordial truth ((1)) is the condition of possibility of truth in the specific sense.[37] If we elaborate on this, we might claim that the transcendental structure of truth (openness, primoridal truth) introduces some universal limitations, as to which propositions we will be justified in assuming to be true.

The problem about this interpretation is epistemological. We do not, within the framework of the historicity of understanding, have an unhistorical (non-relative) access to "Dasein"'s Being. On the contrary, because of "Dasein"'s historicity we always have different possible interpretations, "Weil das Dasein seiner eigenen Existenz nach geschichtlich ist, sind die Zugangsmöglichkeiten und die Auslegungsweisen des Seienden selbst in verschiedenen geschichtlichen Lagen verschieden, variabel".[38] Furthermore, there is no Being unless "Dasein" understands this Being (which in our terminology becomes: without the interpretations of "Dasein", sentences are meaningless), and hence "Dasein" has no access to ahistorical (privileged) truths about its own Being. Accordingly, any attempt to ground the ahistorical truth of propositions in this Being could never become more than the hopeful postulate that it (this Being) was constant (though this fact would remain epistemically out of reach). Finally, the later Heidegger introduces a concept of the history of Being, that is, Being is relativized, making (iv) an implausible candidate for the sort of argument Heidegger needs to avoid relativism. Thus, Heidegger's speaks of "...der...Geschichte der Entbergung des »Sinnes« dessen, was wir das Sein nennen..." in "Vom Wesen der Wahrheit".[39] Simultaneously, truth is linked so intimately to Being that, corresponding to the history of Being, there is a history of truth, a "Geschehen der Wahrheit".[40]

It might be possible to maintain a weaker interpretation of (iv), according to which the history of Being is a continuous process, limiting the leeway of possible projections. This thesis is found in Gadamer, and is connected to his introduction of the concept "effective history" (Wirkungsgeschichte).[41] The point is that any new projection will always have to presuppose previous projections (eg. previous predications of some concept), and hence any projection will be limited by the history of interpretations (eg. by the rules according to which some predicate has been attributed to entities in the past). However, this argument turns out to be insufficient. Firstly, the relativist is not about to deny that the leeway is limited. Secondly, this argument only pertains to one tradition/horizon of meaning, not cross-cultural comparison.

And thirdly, it is not even adequate within one tradition. The sort of continuity Gadamer needs is the existence of common elements (for example truth-values, or "meanings") in any two given horizons within one tradition. But, the existence of common elements between horizons A and B, and horizons B and C, doesn't imply the existence of common elements between horizons A and C. In other words, we are not dealing with a *transitive* relation.

IV

We have defined Heidegger's relativism as (a) the possibility of ascribing different truth-values to the same proposition, within different horizons of meaning, with (b) no objective way of privileging one ascribtion above the other ((a) corresponds to (A), and (b) to (B)). Heidegger does, as we have seen, speak of different, variable projections, and we have argued that given this much he has no way of avoiding the possibility of ascribing differing truth-values. Now, Heidegger might claim that we have objective criteria to "sort out" between beliefs, but this doesn't seem plausible, given the thesis of historicity.

These are the three theses, that have enabled us to conclude that Heidegger's concept of truth implies relativism:

(R1) Uncovering entities presupposes a simultaneous openness and closedness.
(R2) The concept of specific truth is lost in Heidegger.
(R3) We cannot give an ahistorical account of Being.

(R3) implies that Being cannot sufficiently limit the leeway of possible projections. (R1) makes the ascription of different truth-values to the same proposition possible. (R2) makes Heidegger unable to claim that truth is unique, that there are no different (incompatible) truths. If, for instance, he had a truth theory of the following nature:

(C) "p" is true, if and only if, "p" corresponds to a fact (p)

he would have an argument against relativism. But, as we have seen, Heidegger rejects the traditional correspondence theory, and doesn't come up with any specific alternative.

(R3) seems to be implicit in *SuZ*, but becomes more explicit in the later works. Now, in this connexion, Gethmann unfolds the following dilemma for Heidegger: “Nimmt man an, dass die spätphilosophie Heideggers selbst ein Ergebnis der fortschreitenden Seinsvergessenheit ist, ist diese Philosophie nicht kompetent, Aussagen über die Seinsgeschichte zu machen. Nimmt man an, dass die Philosophie Heideggers ausserhalb dieser Entwicklung steht, dann gilt nicht mehr die These, alles Philosophieren sei seinsgeschichtlich bedingt”.[42] So, either we must claim that Heidegger’s thesis of the historicity of Being is, itself, subject to the historicity of Being, and thus we have no reason to take it very seriously, or, we have to claim that the thesis is excluded from the domain of the historicity of Being (is ahistorical, given from God’s point of view), but this would undermine the thesis. I agree with this last point. However, I cannot see that the first horn of the dilemma states a necessity. Gethmann’s underlying epistemic premise seems to be that it is only whatever is absolutely (ahistorically) certain, that we have reason to take seriously. But if this were the case, both the history of philosophy and the history of science would look very problematic, because far too much would have been taken seriously. Of course, the question is if we are ever in the epistemic situation Gethmann seems to require. Still, Gethmann’s point might be read as a more radical version of the reflexive or self-referential paradox, according to which the position we have attributed to Heidegger, cannot be held without contradiction. A more thorough discussion of that interpretation is not within the limits of this paper. Other arguments, that would have to be considered to test the coherence of relativism, would include the Davidsonian objection already mentioned, and considerations of possible candidates for objective criteria of theory choice, by which one could privilege beliefs across different horizons.[43]

Notes

1. For example Dummett, see Dummett, Michael (1978) *Truth and Other Enigmas* (Massachusetts, Duckworth).
2. Horwich has recently supported this view in Horwich, Paul (1990) *Truth* (Oxford, Basil Blackwell).
3. Notice that even though philosophers of science like Kuhn have been classified as relativists, Kuhn is not a relativist in the sense of relativism defined by (A) and (B). Kuhn claims that two theories are incommensurable if the meaning of one theory cannot be stated within the concepts of the other, see Kuhn, Thomas (1970) *The Structure of Scientific Revolutions* (Chicago, The University of Chicago Press). However, if the meaning of one theory cannot be stated within the other, we can’t ascribe the *same* theory different truth-values.

4. Of course there might be a difference between communities defined semantically and spatio-temporally, but we shall presuppose that they have identical extensions. Even if this is not the case, it won't be significant for the thesis we are exploring in this paper.
5. Heidegger, Martin (1986) *Sein und Zeit* (Tübingen, Max Niemeyer Verlag), p. 214.
6. In J. Macquarrie & E. Robinson's translation of *SuZ* "Erschlossenheit" is translated to "disclosedness", (1962) *Being and Time* (Oxford, Basil Blackwell). However, I shall use "open" and "openness" to signify Erschlossen / Erschlossenheit, partly because it makes what I have to say sound less awkward (because of the terminology), partly because I think the translation itself is less awkward.
7. See *SuZ*, p. 151.
8. See Heidegger, Martin (1989) *Die Grundprobleme der Phänomenologie* (Gesamtausgabe band 24) (Frankfurt a.M., Vittorio Klostermann), p. 95.
9. In Tugendhat we find similar tendencies towards a semantic interpretation of Being, e.g. in Tugendhat, Ernst (1989) *Selbstbewusstsein und Selbstbestimmung* (Frankfurt a.M., Suhrkamp), p. 169.
10. Some interpreters, however, claim that it is exclusively, or at least primarily, its own Being to which Dasein is open (amongst these are Theunissen, and Tugendhat in *Selbstbewusstsein und Selbstbestimmung*). We claim that it is Being generally, to which it is open, and that this is the *condition of possibility* of any interpretation, including of Dasein itself. Some of the advantages in this interpretation are pointed out in Lübcke, P. (1981) Die Zweideutigkeit der »Daseins-Formel« beim jungen Heidegger, *Danish Yearbook of Philosophy*, 18.
11. See *SuZ*, p. 216-219.
12. *SuZ*, p. 218.
13. *SuZ*, p. 223.
14. Heidegger, Martin (1976) *Logik. Die Frage nach der Wahrheit* (Gesamtausgabe, band 21) (Frankfurt a.M., Vittorio Klostermann), p. 144.
15. See *SuZ*, p. 219.
16. See *SuZ*, p. 221.
17. Earlier in *SuZ* openness is defined by thrownness, projection and discourse (Rede) (p. 161-162). Why is discourse left out at this point? The most plausible explanation seems to be that discourse, in which meaning is articulated, is a projection- and thrownness-immanent structure, because Dasein is thrown into, and projects upon, a horizon of meaning. For a longer discussion of this, see Herrmann, Friedrich von (1985) *Subjekt und Dasein* (Frankfurt a.M., Vittorio Klostermann).
18. See *SuZ*, p. 222.
19. See Tugendhat, Ernst (1970) *Der Wahrheitsbegriff bei Husserl und Heidegger* (Berlin, Walter de Gruyter & Co.).
20. *SuZ*, p. 218.
21. See *SuZ*, p. 224-225.
22. This is in accordance with the following: "Wenn innerweltliches Seiendes mit dem Sein des Daseins entdeckt, das heisst zu Verständnis gekommen ist, sagen wir, es hat Sinn", *SuZ*, p. 151, and "Was im verstehenden Erschliessen artikulierbar ist, nennen wir Sinn", *SuZ*, p. 151.
23. Here, we don't mean to forward a position that, as in the philosophy of the logical positivists, identifies conditions of verifiability with possible verifying/falsifying sense-experiences. A modern anti-realism/verificationism will build on a more refined picture of procedures of verification, see, amongst others, Dummett, M. (1978) The Philosophical Basis of Intuitionistic Logic, in: *Truth and Other Enigmas*, p. 227.

24. *SuZ*, p. 226.
25. See Davidson, D. (1984) A Coherence Theory of Truth and Knowledge, in: E. LePore (Ed) *Truth and Interpretation* (Oxford, Basil Blackwell), p. 307. (However, Davidson has adopted a rather different truth-theory recently, see Davidson, D. (1990) The Structure and Content of Truth, *The Journal of Philosophy*, LXXXVII.
26. The correspondence theory is possible if, in those cases where p can be verified, we explain this by p's independently being true. But this, of course, would have to make us give up an anti-realist interpretation.
27. See Figal, Günter (1988) *Martin Heidegger. Phänomenologie der Freiheit* (Frankfurt a.M., Athenäum), p. 43.
28. Figal, Günter *Martin Heidegger. Phänomenologie der Freiheit*, p. 43.
29. Tugendhat, E. *Der Wahrheitsbegriff bei Husserl und Heidegger*, p. 331.
30. I deny the possibility of *subjective* relativism in advance. Theunissen gives an interpretation of the analysis of Dasein, according to which it implies subjectivism (see Theunissen, Michael (1965) *Der Andere* (Berlin, Walter de Gruyter & Co.)), but he isn't able to account for the fundamental connexion between Dasein and Mitdasein. Dasein is constituted by (wouldn't exist without) Mitdasein, with which it shares the same world (Welt), that is, the same horizon of concepts. Dasein has been handed down (überliefern) a world from Mitdasein, without which, it wouldn't be Dasein.
31. See Tennant, N. (1981) Is This a Proof I See Before Me?, *Analysis*, 41, and Dummett, Michael (1978) The Philosophical Basis of Intuitionistic Logic, in: *Truth and Other Enigmas*, p. 225.
32. See Dummett, M. (1978) Wittgenstein's Philosophy of Mathematics, in: *Truth and Other Enigmas*.
33. See Wright, C. (1987) Second Thoughts about Criteria, in: C. Wright *Realism, Meaning and Truth* (Oxford, Basil Blackwell), p. 279.
34. See Wright, C. Second Thoughts about Criteria, p. 275.
35. See Davidson, D. (1984) On the Very Idea of a Conceptual Scheme, in: Davidson, Donald *Inquiries into Truth and Interpretation* (Oxford, Oxford University Press).
36. Alternatives to the principle of charity are suggested by D. Lewis and R. Grandy. They hold, respectively, "an improved principle of charity" and "the principle of humanity". See Lewis, D. (1974) Radical Interpretation, *Synthese*, 27, p. 336, and Grandy, R. (1973) Reference, Meaning and Belief, *The Journal of Philosophy*, LXX, p. 443.
37. See Gethmann, Carl Friedrich *Verstehen und Auslegung* (Bonn, Bouvier Verlag Herbert Grundmann), p. 323.
38. *Die Grundprobleme der Phänomenologie*, p. 30.
39. Heidegger, Martin (1978) *Wegmarken* (Frankfurt a.M., Vittorio Klostermann), p. 198.
40. See Heidegger, Martin (1986) *Der Ursprung des Kunstwerkes* (Stuttgart, Reclam), p. 73.
41. See Gadamer, Hans-Georg (1975) *Wahrheit und Methode* (Tübingen, J.C.B. Mohr (Paul Siebeck)), p. 284-290.
42. Gethmann, C.F. *Verstehen und Auslegung*, p. 321.
43. I would like to thank Poul Lübcke for his always relevant and insightful comments on an earlier draft of this paper, and on the work that preceded. Also, I would like to thank Finn Collin on the editorial board of *Danish Yearbook of Philosophy*, who has given valuable suggestions for improvements.

Danish Yearbook of Philosophy, Vol. **27** (1992), 23-43

TACIT KNOWING, GESTALT THEORY, AND THE MODEL OF PERCEPTUAL CONSCIOUSNESS

Robert E Innis
University of Massachussets-Lowell
University of Copenhagen

Although he began his work in the theory of knowledge with a reflection upon the social matrices of science, a topic which has moved to the forefront in recent discussions,[1] Michael Polanyi realized that his treatment of the many issues involved in this important but relatively restricted theme would force him to deal with the structures of knowing quite generally. The peculiarity of his later work, however, is that it did not arise out of a specifically philosophical framework but from what Polanyi saw as some general implications of certain elements proper to the model of knowing developed by Gestalt theory, particularly in its 'classic' phase.[2] What we have in Polanyi's mature work is, in fact, a transposition of Gestalt theory into a general theory of knowledge and its application to a range of data that covered practically the whole field of human cognitional process, ranging from sense perception to the construction of art works and mythico-religious structures.[3]

Indeed, while Gestalt theory formed the starting point of and permanent point of reference for Polanyi's general epistemological project, there are at the same time remarkable and highly instructive divergences in the two operations, and it would not be correct to think that Polanyi, any more than, say, Merleau-Ponty, merely dressed up some components of empirical psychology in epistemological clothing. I want on this occasion to chart the nature of Polanyi's appropriation and use of Gestalt theory, to show how his epistemological project went beyond the confines of Gestalt theory, and to indicate its heuristic fertility in our own attempts to thematize the fundamental lines of cognitional process.

By studying how Polanyi's epistemological project went beyond the confines of Gestalt theory as such I hope to expose the essential contours of his own epistemological model, its fundamental novelty, and selected points of intersection with parallel projects and present problems.[4]

I. *The Structural Analogy between Knowledge and Skills*

The pivot of Polanyi's theory of knowledge, the thread that runs throughout all the various expositions of his model of mind and mental processes, is "the structural analogy between knowledge and skill" ('Knowing and Being,' KB 130). What is this structural analogy and upon what base of examples does it depend?

It is a well-known fact of everyday experience that a motoric achievement such as walking a tight-rope or performing on the parallel bars is a feat of coordination.

What is being coordinated?

Obviously, a set of actions and movements. Now the feat of coordination involves bringing these movements to bear upon the performance that one has in mind and that lies at the focus of our attention. This bringing to bear is, Polanyi noted, a process of 'integration' wherein the particular movements, accessible kinesthetically and (to speak in phenomenological terms) prethematically, are brought into a unity: the completed performance itself as a 'comprehensive entity.' We know from experience that in the performance of motoric skills we can paralyze the action as a whole if we concentrate on the constituent actions in themselves, keeping them, rather than the task at hand, at the center of one's attention, a process called "destructive analysis" by Polanyi. We have to *rely* on the actions and feelings, use them in an instrumental manner, commit ourselves 'uncritically' to them. As Polanyi put it in terms of conscious functions, we must 'attend from' these particulars while 'attending to' what we are doing. This incipient 'from-to' structure, espied in numerous other instances, will become the structural key to Polanyi's whole epistemology and the source of its immense, but undervalued and neglected, heuristic fertility.

The recognition of a physiognomy – a face or its moods, for instance, but also the 'facies' of diseases and of species of insects and flowers – manifests a similar structure. In Polanyi's reckoning the various features of the face, symptoms of the disease, characteristics of the insect or flower function as a not completely specifiable and complex set of clues on which we have to rely in order to recognize – in an act resembling Peircean abduction and the types of processes now being charted in non-linear systems – the face, mood, disease, insect, or flower. We do not, according to Polanyi, go, in summative fashion, from one isolated item to another and from their collection, as necessary and sufficient conditions, 'deduce' the object. Rather, we attend, for example, 'from' the features 'to' the face or the mood. We do not focus on the features in themselves but rely on them, in the same fashion as we rely on our consciousness of our bodily movements for achieving a coherent action. Just as we can bring an action to a halt by turning our attention to its constituent particulars, so focussing our attention on the particulars of visual wholes such as those mentioned above, but easily extended to line drawings, geometrical figures, and so forth, will cause them to disintegrate phenomenally as unities.

A third paradigmatic example, exploited also by Merleau-Ponty in a way that parallels Polanyi's, is the use of a probe by a blind man or, with appropriate modifications, by a surgeon or dentist. Here we have an illustration of another important aspect of this from-to structure. A probe is first of all an object external to our body and we can *feel* it as external to us by attending *to* the pressure of it on our hand. However, we do not use the probe in order to feel *it*, but to feel by means of it, using it as an instrument. It has, as Heidegger saw clearly and continued to emphasize, an *um ... zu* structure.[5] When we no longer directly and objectively feel the probe in our hands and fingers but ourselves feel what the probe itself is touching so that we come to know this object both 'directly' and 'mediately,' we can then be said to be attending *from* the pressures and impacts made by the probe on our body *to* what these pressures and impacts *mean*. That is, we have to bring these pressures and impacts to bear on a focus, on an object or comprehensive entity, through an act of 'integration.'

Now, in performing these integrative acts – and others like them – Polanyi thinks that we either rely on or come into possession of, achieve, a kind of knowledge that we cannot put into words, a kind of knowledge, that is, in short, 'tacit,' 'unspecifiable,' 'inarticulate,' 'unformalizable.' This tacit character is especially obvious in such cases as bicycle riding, swimming, walking, speaking, where we are not aware, except after long and difficult analyses of something that we do easily, of the rules or laws we are obeying in performing an action. This, of course, has long been one of Chomsky's main points. Likewise, the actual, operative topographic knowledge of the human body possessed by a surgeon in itself inarticulate, although it may rely on a detailed and complex articulate mapping of the human body. This knowledge, Polanyi contends, is the result of a massive preconceptual act of integration, a feat of imagination built up over the course of long dealing with the three-dimensional internal structure of the human body. No sum of direct, explicit knowledge or awareness of the discrete parts will generate the three-dimensional – relational – Gestalt which is the image of the human body. Rather, once again, we must say that the surgeon must attend *from* these discrete items *to* their integrating center. Otherwise, we will have no 'praxical' grasp of the structure itself. Both, therefore, the bicycle rider and the surgeon are in possession of tacit knowledge, and what they can *say* about this knowledge is in itself inadequate to transmit it, which can only be done by practice and initiation. The differentiation, therefore, between 'theoretical' and 'practical' surgery that characterized the Medieval medical faculty is an epistemological monstrosity or at least curiosity. Articulate formal statements – which may indeed be possible and certainly desirable – are meant only to guide us into the realm itself, to function, as Polanyi put it, as *maxims* which have to be applied in the concrete consciousness of the knower.[6]

Let us turn to the systematic point of these examples.

First of all, we note a distinction in the two ways of being conscious. One way is being directly aware of an item in itself – paying attention to a movement, a line, a patch of color, an articulate clue. A second way is to direct one's attention away from the item, so to speak, in the direction to which it is pointing, that is, to rely on this item, being conscious of it, to be sure, but attending 'from' it 'to' something else. The item in this case has an essentially 'indexical' character. This *from-consciousness* is called by Polanyi 'subsidiary' awareness, while *to-consciousness* is called 'focal awareness.' Thus, "subsidiary awareness and focal awareness are mutually exclusive... .Our attention can hold only one focus at a time and ... it would hence be self-contradictory to be both subsidiarily and focally aware of the same particulars at the same time" (PK 56-57). The particulars upon which we rely, be they movements, lines, anatomical slices, feelings and pressures, symbolically formulated clues, and the wholes or intelligible unities which they compose, are, therefore, terms of different structures of consciousness.

Secondly, the differences between these two forms of consciousness is, in Polanyi's use of the term, 'logical.' They are irreducible to one another, in such fashion that shifting attention to a previously subsidiarily attended-to item will destroy the coherence to which it is contributory or cause it to change its appearance and its function in the full cognitional performance. Polanyi calls this a case of 'logical integration.' It is this from-to structure, inherent in the logical structure of skills, that is the foundation of the structural analogy between knowledge and skill. "The structural kinship of the arts of knowing and doing is indeed such that they are rarely exercised in isolation; we usually meet a blend of the two....Though we may prefer to speak of *understanding* a comprehensive object or situation and of *mastering* a skill, we do use the two words nearly as synonyms" ('Knowing and Being,' KB 126). It is because of this, consequently, that in *Personal Knowledge* Polanyi can say that the unspecifiability of skills is "closely associated to the findings of Gestalt psychology....The classic theme of Gestalt psychology ... is that the particulars of a pattern or a tune must be apprehended jointly, for if you observe the particulars separately they form no pattern or tune" (PK 55-57).

Thirdly, it is clear that the distinction between focal and subsidiary awareness functions within an 'integrative matrix': skilful knowing and doing proceed by integrations or syntheses of particulars into wholes of various sorts. These integrations, as exemplified in the foregoing instances, are intentional performances, involving in these cases the personal participation of the cognitive agent. It is this model of a tacit integration – first of all in the perceptual realm – that Polanyi uses extensively in his further cognitional analyses. Indeed, according to Polanyi, it is only by adverting to the 'intentional' character of integrative performances that the logical structure of tacit knowing appears, and it is this aspect of the problem that Polanyi finds overlooked in Gestalt theory. "The logical structure is not apparent in the automatic perception of visual and auditory wholes from which Gestalt psychology has derived its prevailing generalizations" (PK 57).

What, then, in more detail, is Polanyi's model of perception, how does it function as a model for the logic of discovery, and how is it related to Gestalt theory's analysis of perception?

II. *Perception and the Logic of Discovery*

In Polanyi's cognitional model, perception, itself modelled on the structure of a skilful achievement, always functions as the chief paradigm for understanding knowing as such. What was capital in this paradigm was the necessity of the integrative act, an intentional performance, which produced the coherent object of consciousness, whether, in a more extended sense, that coherent object was what was effected in motoric action, construed in visual perception, pointed to in verbal denotation, and so forth. In fact, as we will see, Polanyi thought he could discern throughout all the operations of consciousness a universal 'triadic structure,' composed of subsidiarily intended particulars, the focally attended-to whole or unity, and the tacit act that held them together.

Now the central thesis of Gestalt theory, in the form with which Polanyi was most familiar, is that primary experience, prior to reflective analysis, is not a mosaic of sensations but a field of 'wholes' or forms (Gestalten) governed by definite laws of organization which are intrinsic to sensory processes as such. The field of wholes is composed first of all of sensory wholes, understood generally either in terms of visual wholes or auditory wholes, the latter being von Ehrenfels' original concern. However, as Köhler writes, "from our present point of view ... sensory organization appears as a primary fact which arises from the elementary dynamics of the nervous system" (GP 118), a position echoed far and wide in cognitive psychology and many 'materialist' epistemologies. Or, as Köhler put it in *The Place of Values in a World of Facts*:

> In Gestalt psychology we distinguish three major traits which are conspicuous in all cases of specific organization or gestalt. Phenomenally the world is neither an indifferent mosaic nor an indifferent continuum. It exhibits definite segregated units or contexts in all degrees of complexity, articulation and clearness. Secondly, such units show properties belonging to them as contexts or systems. Again, the parts of such units or contexts exhibit dependent properties in the sense that, given the place of a part in the context, its dependent properties are determined by this position (85).

The same point is made, more generally, in a passage in *Gestalt Psychology*:

> Gestalt psychology holds [that] sensory units have acquired names, have become richly symbolic, and are now known to have certain practical uses, while nevertheless they have existed as units before any of these further facts were added. Gestalt psychology claims that it is precisely the original segregation of circumscribed wholes which makes it possible for the sensory world to appear so utterly imbued with meaning to the adult; for, in the gradual entrance into the sensory field, meaning follows the lines drawn by natural organization; it usually enters into segregated wholes (82).

How does Polanyi's model stand with respect to notions such as these?

Already in *The Logic of Liberty* (1951) and in *Science, Faith and Society* (1946[1964]) Polanyi was insisting on the interpreted character of all contents of consciousness, limning in fact in its essential contours a distinctively 'hermeneutical' model of perception in particular and of consciousness itself in general. "The moment we notice a thing, say by sight, we perceive it *as* something....Such facts as these leave little scope for sensations as primarily given data. They show that even at the most elementary stages of cognition, we are already committing ourselves to an act of interpretation" (LL 19). Indeed, as Polanyi wrote in *The Study of Man*, Gestalt theory had "missed an aspect of its subject which I believe to be decisive for our understanding of knowledge and for our corresponding appreciation of man's position in the universe" (28-29).

What has Gestalt theory missed?

It has "described our perception of Gestalt as a passive experience," while Polanyi's view is that the only proper model of knowing is one in which it is seen that knowledge is "shaped by the knower's personal action" (SM 28). Polanyi rejects the notion that spontaneous equilibration of neural traces is satisfactory to explain knowing. For him Gestalt is "the outcome of an active shaping of experience performed in the pursuit of knowledge. This shaping or integrating I hold to be the great indispensable tacit power by which all knowledge is discovered and, once discovered, is held to be true" (SM 6).

Secondly, "having realized that personal participation predominates both in the area of tacit and explicit knowledge, we are ready to transpose the findings of Gestalt-psychology into a theory of knowledge: a theory based primarily on the analysis of comprehension" (SM 29). This personal participation is, for Polanyi, a consequence of the intentional effort needed to cross what he calls the 'logical gap' between clues, or subsidiarily intended particulars quite generally, and the focus upon which they bear. This notion of a logical gap is crucial for understanding the personal character of tacit knowing and of properly heuristic acts. *That* there is a gap is not apparent in what seems to be cases of automatic perceptual organization. But without the distinction between focal and subsidiary awareness, considered as a 'logical' distinction, the gap is not properly seen, although it is apparent in the distinction between attention and comprehension, since we can 'attend' to a field of data without being able to 'construe' it. The act of construal, whether prearticulate or articulate, is the tacit act of integration for Polanyi. Still, while the initial movement from perceptual clues to a perceptual focus is a performance, the movement from an articulate expression to a field of experience upon which it bears also involves crossing a logical gap, since, on Polanyi's reckoning, formalization must always remain incomplete, and denotative acts, that is, acts of applying a formalism, always have an element of essential indeterminacy about them.

As Polanyi put it:

> ... in all applications of a formalism to experience there is an indeterminacy involved, which must be resolved by the observer on the grounds of unspecifiable criteria. Now we may say further that the process of applying a language to things is also necessarily unformalized: that it is inarticulate. Denotation, then, is an art, and whatever we say about things assumes our endorsement of our own skill in practicing this art. This personal coefficient of all affirmation (is) inherent in the use of language (PK 81).

It is clear, then, that the notion of 'logical gap' transcends the purely perceptual realm, for, in human knowing and living, specifically articulate clues, functioning in representational and symbolic schemes, point toward foci which are not themselves perceptually visible. In mathematics, the formal discipline *par excellence*, invention cannot come from following a detailed specific set of rules but only from looking toward the unknown, in George Polya's[7] sense, upon which the formal symbolically organized elements bear. Likewise, there is, in general, a gap between the physical characteristics of a script and the meaning or conceptual focus borne by the script. The so-called transparency of language is just an explicit parallel to the transparency of a probe, tool, or instrument that we have embodied ourselves in and interiorized. Now, the reality of the logical gap is established by the reality of the distinction between focal and subsidiary awareness. Classical Gestalt theory lacked this fundamental distinction.

Thirdly, "the lesson derived from perception" has to be applied "generally to the pursuit of knowledge by scientific inquiry" ('The Unaccountable Element in Science,' KB 117). In fact, "the logic of perceptual integration may serve ... as a model for the logic of discovery" ('The Logic of Tacit Inference,' KB 139). As Polanyi put it, "the structure of scientific intuition is the same as perception. Intuition, thus defined, is not more mysterious than perception – but not less mysterious either" ('The Unaccountable Element in Science,' KB 118). What structure do the two processes have in common?

> The advancement of science consists in discerning Gestalten that are aspects of reality. We know that perception selects, shapes, and assimilates clues by a process not explicitly controlled by the perceiver. Since the powers of scientific discerning are of the same kind as those of perception, they too operate by selecting, shaping and assimilating clues without focally attending to them (SFS 11).

Now in empirical science these clues are embedded in a formal, theoretical, and experimental, that is, praxical, matrix which is considerably more complicated than the matrices of perception. Nevertheless, the recognition of a scientific Gestalt – a pattern or regularity in sub-atomic processes, a frequency obtaining in a set of events, a functional relation between a set of organs, a significant historical or sociological correlation, and so forth – brings into operation integrative powers similar to those of perception, and just as we have to indwell the clues in perceptual processes, so we indwell the articulate, formal clues of scientific inquiry, which, in effect, become parts of our 'intentional' body (cf. Holton on themata[8]).

There are few parallels in Gestalt theory to these notions except for the paradigmatic role of perception and the insistence upon primary organization. At the same time Polanyi did not want to deny the empirical facts to which Gestalt theory appealed, nor its favorite examples. Polanyi's hesitation was with the interpretation and analysis of the facts. Rather, Polanyi wanted to develop, in a way similar to Merleau-Ponty, who, in Polanyi's opinion, lacked a differentiated notion of tacit integrations, a doctrine of the originary dynamic intentionality of consciousness, rooted in the body and perception, to be sure, but extending to the higher forms of organization, too.

Fourthly, when Polanyi speaks of the *logic* of discovery he does not mean that discovery is the result of following consistently a set of formal rules or that it is, in the strict sense of the term, a 'logical' process. By 'logic' in this context he really means 'structure' and what he was concerned to show is that discovery follows a 'tacit logic' that *relies* subsidiarily on formal rules and procedures for arriving at a conclusion. Indeed, the rules function as *maxims* operating in the cognitional praxis of the cognitive agent. These maxims or concrete rules define and constitute the skill of the cognitive agent, and, as we saw, in all skills there is a tacit preconceptual component as well as a performative, personal element.

Fifthly, Polanyi writes that "the conditions in which discovery usually occurs and the general way of its happening certainly show it to be a process of emergence rather than a feat of operative action" (SFS 33). In support of this experiential point Polanyi draws, not uncritically, upon the work in heuristics of Poincaré and Hadamard and their delineation of the four stages composing the grammar of discovery: preparation, incubation, illumination, verification (see Polanyi PK 120-131 for a detailed discussion of what is presented here in shorthand).

The process of preparation corresponds in fact, although Polanyi does not make the connection, to the old Scholastic notion of disposing the phantasm (*dispositio phantasmatum*) or to the more contemporary idea of manipulating the (basically symbolic) elements of a problem so that they are in the proper form for eliciting the insight from and into them, a theme that lies at the heart of Bernard Lonergan's cognitional theory, which has multiple affinities with that of Polanyi.[9] The period of incubation is the equivalent to a latent period after the strenuous intentional effort of the process of preparation, where we are not consciously or directly thinking of the problem itself. The event of illumination, the solution – or proposed solution to a problem, which is itself manifested as an 'intellectual desire' – comes as a release to the prior tension of inquiry, but, of itself, comes effortlessly, as something that happens to us, spontaneously. But the passivity here is something quite different from the passivity of the Gestalt theorists, for the event is not non-deliberate, but emerges within a matrix of intense intentional striving to cross the logical gap. The point is that it does not come automatically by means of a process of spontaneous equilibration but as a process of emergence, of fundamental novelty. With each novel act a new meaning, or new form of meaning, arises in the world. Thus there is a fairly direct line from the grammar of discovery to the later general notion of meaning in Polanyi's epistemology. The process or stage of verification follows upon the proposal of a solution, which in itself may not be veridical. Hence it has to be checked by crossing once again a logical gap between the formal solution and the field of data upon which it putatively bears. This common structure of crossing a logical gap constitutes "the essential kinship between heuristics and verification" (SFS 29).

Once again, then, we see Polanyi's insistence upon performance, upon commitment, upon intentional action coming to the fore. This act is, in the last analysis, an act of which we can be aware only in an unreflecting manner, since in the very act of comprehending we live in the act itself (SM 14). Becoming conscious of our acts, therefore, means adverting to them in reflection by attending to authentic performances and their embodiment in objective matrices. Thus, Polanyi has no intention of supplying or trying to discover an algorithm for generating discoveries, for there are none, though there are rules functioning as maxims upon which we can rely. What he wanted to do was to pin down the grammar of discovery and to show how it contributes to our understanding of the structure of the human mind as such.[10]

Having studied the analogies between perception and discovery, it is now possible to extend even further our investigation and to delineate more thematically the nature of higher forms of integration which manifest the creative powers of man. Language and all articulate forms constitute higher level Gestalten, relying on higher forms of integration, and Polanyi wanted his epistemological model to apply also to them. What role, then, does his account of them have in his transformation of Gestalt theory?

III. *Higher Forms of Integration*

In classical Gestalt theory language played very little role, concentrating as it did on primary perceptual processes. But although Polanyi took perception and the logic of perceptual integrations as his primary model for constructing a general theory of knowledge, he had no intention of arguing that knowing is just a variant – on the same level – of perception. In fact, he had a rather different view of the matter. Consider the following text:

> All human thought comes into existence by grasping the meaning and mastering the use of language. Little of our mind lives in our natural body; a truly human intellect dwells in us only when our lips shape words and our eyes read print.[11]

At the same time, "the logic of language itself – the way language is used – remains tacit. Indeed, it is easy to see that the structure of tacit knowing contains a general theory of meaning which applies also to language."[12] More generally, "speech has the fundamental structure of all meaningful uses of consciousness in animals and men."[13]

This fundamental structure is, we know, composed of focal and subsidiary awareness and tacit integrating acts of consciousness. How do these elements in Polanyi's epistemology apply to the realms of language and meaning?

The semantic aspect of tacit knowing, that is, our capacity to read clues and cues of all sorts as signs pointing toward a meaning which is a coherent whole, can be extended, Polanyi thought, into the conscious structure of how we understand and produce speech and other expressions. The semantic integrations of tacit consciousness involve, so to speak, a transposition of meaning away from the subsidiarily intended particulars, much in the same way that feeling is transposed out to the end of the probe. The probe is the paradigm of "how an interpretative effort transposes meaningless feelings into meaningful ones, and places these at some distance from the original feeling. We become aware of the feelings in our hand in terms of their meaning located at the tip of the probe or stick to which we are attending" (TD 12-13). In our encounter with spoken or written language, or signs and symbols in general, we are able, in Polanyi's view, to bring them to bear on a focus which is their meaning. Language – as a system of representational signs – is the intentional equivalent of a probe extending and transforming our bodily equipment beyond the limits of our own body. Indeed, just as we dwell in our own body and attend to the world by integrating it in certain ways, so by integrating certain physical sounds and marks we attend to the world in novel ways, too.

The world thus produced and grasped is a properly semantic Gestalt. The subsidiarily intended particulars – the flow of experience and the system of representational signs – are apprehended as supporting or pointing to a conceptual focus, which is the articulate focal meaning itself. The sense-endowing act – cognate to Husserl's ensouling act – is now indispensably operating within the explicit formal matrix, for without it the signs and the meanings toward which they point fall apart, giving us once again a case of logical disintegration. Thus, in addition to a tacit power which generates the focus there is also a necessary tacit coefficient which must always be present to keep the articulate focus in existence and to control its application (SFS 13). The tacit power itself is fundamentally a combinatorial power: "To speak is to *contrive* signs, to *observe* their fitness, and to *interpret* their alternative relations; though the animal possesses each of these three faculties, he cannot combine them" (PK 82).

Word, sentence, paragraph, discourse make up one complex, stratified, articulate Gestalt, and we see here, quite clearly, the extensiveness of Polanyi's generalization of Gestalt theory. Further, it is clear that in Gestalt theory, as well as in Polanyi's epistemology as whole, perceptual classification involves recognition of *types*, and thus that there is an incipient generalization taking place outside the confines of language itself. The text previously cited from Köhler concerning the segregation of reality into units is, to a great degree, correct, but, on Polanyi's view, it is not the whole story. For although language follows the lines of perception in certain respects – since perception uncovers real Gestalten which are aspects of reality – perception, and the segregation of significant units in the world, is also dependent upon language and symbolic-representational schemes, in such a fashion that certain things – Gestalten – cannot be perceived or experienced until a symbolic representation of them has been devised, as, for example, in the use of maps, charts, and graphs.[14] Perceptual experience and language do not run along completely parallel but interpenetrate and interact upon one another. Language – and other articulate forms – does not fit *over* the perceptual world; it fits *into* it, so much so that 'word' and 'object' arise together. The object that arises, however, is an articulate object, a conceptual Gestalt borne by the subsidiarily apprehended and indwelt representational scheme.

In these notions Polanyi is closer to the positions found in the classic works of Sapir (and to lesser degree of Whorf) and other cognate positions such as the recent work of Lakoff and Johnson on the 'linguistic constitution of the world' than to properly Gestalt analyses.[15] Consequently, he argues for a certain form of the linguistic relativity thesis. As he put it:

> Different languages are alternative conclusions, arrived at by the secular gropings of different groups of people at different periods of history. They sustain alternative conceptual frameworks, interpreting all things that can be talked about in terms of somewhat different allegedly recurrent features (PK 112).[16]

If such is the case, then denotation is an art or a skill.

> To classify things in terms of features form which we have names, as we do in talking about things, requires the same kind of connoisseurship as the naturalist must have for identifying specimens of plants or animals. Thus the art of speaking precisely, by applying a rich vocabulary exactly, resembles the delicate discrimination practised by the expert taxonomist (PK 81).

The use of an articulate instrument, therefore, is identical in structure with perceptual processes, though it obviously cannot be reduced to perception as such.

In Polanyi's later writings there is an effort to apply the general triadic structure – the ultimate generalization of the Gestalt model – to non-linguistic forms of expression as well as to properly aesthetic linguistic objects: poems, plays, metaphors, and so forth. This is done especially in the last book *Meaning*, where Polanyi's thoughts range over all the arts and extend even to myth and religion. In these higher forms of articulation, made fundamentally possible by the original feat of articulation, man produces vast edifices of meaning in which he dwells. Here Polanyi speaks of a logic of self-integration into these Gestalten, where the role of the subsidiaries becomes even more crucial, for it is the specific *intrinsically interesting* character of the subsidiaries themselves – as aspects of our lives – that, in effect, bring ourselves into focus by being brought into a novel unity.

In the realm of articulation as a higher form of integration we see once again the generalizing power of Polanyi's transformation of Gestalt theory. Man can *produce* complex *articulate Gestalten* by the same kind of integrating power at work in perception and skilful achievement. A full human cognitional act involves a combination of acts and levels, so much so that a known *object* can be a highly complex thing, involving perceptual, imaginal, symbolic, and affective components. In this respect Polanyi's epistemology is in close agreement with the classic pragmatist analyses of Peirce and Dewey. Polanyi's notion of an object, identical in one form with that of a meaning, is considerably more complicated an nuanced than that of original Gestalt theory (see the discussion of wholes and meanings in PK 57-58). The later work of Rudolf Arnheim has been fruitful in the aesthetic realm, but it plays no role in the thought of Polanyi himself.

IV. *The Rejection of Isomorphism*

Let us turn now to Polanyi's rejection of the principle of isomorphism as conceived by Gestalt theory. Such a rejection is meant to establish the ontological reality and autonomy of consciousness, in Polanyi's sense of the term, as well as to reject behaviorist and positivist methods in the social and human sciences. I will concentrate exclusively on the first issue.

As formulated by Köhler, the principle of isomorphism lay at the center of the Gestalt model. Writing in *The Place of Values in a World of Facts* Köhler stated: "Isomorphism represents, indeed, the only way in which mental life can be dynamically interpreted, in which it can become a subject-matter of physics" (396). Further, as he says on the following page:

> As far as structure is concerned, the neural correlates of phenomenal experience would have to be strictly isomorphic with such experience, and consequently experience would give us a more direct knowledge of certain aspects of macroscopic dynamics than any physical or physiological approach could ever be expected to yield: because such an approach is indirect under all circumstances (397).

The principle of isomorphism in Köhler's thought functions, in effect, as a postulate and as a heuristic device for further investigations. Köhler did not want to admit any extraneous principles – extraneous ultimately to physical laws, as he understood the term 'physical' – that would account for strictly psychological or phenomenal *experience*, or experience as *observed*. "A genuine theory of observed facts postulates a structure of further explanatory facts" (DP 123) and *these* facts must be properly physiological. The reason for this postulate seems to be a deep-seated desire to maintain the absolute unity of nature and a form of (albeit differentiated) monism.

At the same time, Gestalt theory was always – and still is – an attempt to get at the way experience de facto *appears*, the way it is directly *accessible* to us, without our falling, nevertheless, into the trap of a naive introspectionism. Thus, writes Köhler, "any attempt to construct the correlates of these processes will have to use as their primary evidence the characteristics of such mental facts" (DP 109), and Polanyi himself will appeal to the characteristics of such mental facts. In a later paper, 'Psychology and Evolution,' however, Köhler writes: "it remains to be seen whether principles of action in nature can really be recognized in the way human thinking proceeds. Obviously, if attempts in this direction should end in failure, the postulate of invariance (=isomorphism) could no longer be accepted in its radical form, and a dualistic view of the world would become unavoidable."[17]

In *Science, Faith and Society* Polanyi wrote:

> Köhler assumes that the perception of shapes is caused by the spontaneous reorganization of the physical traces made by sense impressions inside our sense organs. He assumes that these traces somehow interact and coalesce to a dynamic order, the formation of which produces in the observer the perception of a shape (33).

For Polanyi, however, the perception of a shape – whether concrete or abstract – is the paradigm of an emergence, which on the ontological plane "works in the manner of an innovation achieved by tacit integration" (TD 90). Now consciousness for Polanyi cannot under any circumstances be reduced to an epiphenomenal state: it is "logically untenable [that] all conscious mental processes can be interpreted as epiphenomena of a chain of material events occurring in the nervous system" (PK 159). As he put it later on in *Personal Knowledge*: "Some say that we merely speak in two different languages when referring to thought on the one hand and to neural processes on the other. But we speak in two languages because we are talking of two different things" (PK 389). The ground for these assertions is Polanyi's central thesis that "the unspecifiability of a conscious act of comprehension implies the impossibility of accounting for it in terms of a fixed neurological mechanism" (PK 398), for the "neurological model is – like a machine – strictly impersonal and can account for none of the unspecifiable propensities of the subject" (PK 263). These unspecifiable propensities are the principal focus of Polanyi's work.

It is true that Köhler tried to show that there are dynamic elements – field processes – involved in cognitional processes which are not reducible to fixed anatomical or machinelike characters. But at the same time he insisted on the *structural identity* of consciousness and neural states, though they are not, as we saw, equally accessible. Nevertheless, Polanyi's approach was built upon an isomorphism of an entirely different sort, and it allowed him to arrive at radically different conclusions concerning the relations between neural and conscious processes. As he wrote in his paper 'On Body and Mind':

> But I am concerned with the analysis of conscious processes. I can repeat therefore that the bearing by which we understand both the input and the output of a neurological process must be established by ourselves, by our interpretation of the behavioral and neural signs of this input and output. *The neural functions supply these signs, but they do not supply their interpretation.* Since this interpretation forms no part of the nervous system, the system cannot be said to feel, learn, reason, et cetera. These are experiences or actions of the subject using his own neural processes (*The New Scholasticism*, 43 (1969), 202).

The relation between consciousness and neural signs is isomorphic with that between subsidiary and focal awareness. We know that *in* the tacit act of integration we can distinguish two forms of consciousness and these forms have two radically different terms. In the perception of an object – say, a visual object – the two logically distinct terms are the subsidiary particulars and the focally intended whole emerging from their integration by the synthetic act of consciousness which crosses the logical gap.

Now just as there is a logical gap between the particulars and the whole upon which they bear, so there is according to Polanyi's model a logical gap between neural processes and consciousness, both considered as *levels* of systemic processes. The relation between these levels is understood in analogous fashion according to the paradigm of the relations between parts and wholes. Polanyi thinks of the mind as fundamentally the total interpretative integration of the body considered as a subsidiarily intended system. Thus he can speak of the distinction between "the mind as a from-to experience and the subsidiaries of this experience, when seen focally, as a bodily mechanism."[18] As he put it, "the mind harnesses neurophysiological mechanisms; though it depends on them, it is not determined by them."[19] In this sense, then, "mind is the meaning of certain bodily mechanisms; it is lost from view when we look at them focally."[20] Echoing the work of Rothschild, Polanyi asserts that in fact "the mind is the meaning of the body."[21]

Neural processes and conscious processes, accordingly, do not run along parallel tracks but are rather related by a *tacit logic*. This logic is the same whether applied to the structure of cognitional processes or the structure of "stratified entities,"[22] wherein the subsidiary particulars form a lower level that is integrated by an organizing principle. Consciousness is a higher level organizing principle integrating the boundary conditions left open by neurological processes. Thus, as Polanyi put it, in the case of the mind-brain relation:

> We are presented . . . with an ontological counterpart of the *logical disintegration* caused by switching our attention from the integrating centre of a comprehensive entity to its particulars. . . . The logical structure of tacit knowing thus covers in every detail the ontological structure of a combined pair of levels.[23]

On Polanyi's position, consciousness and mind constitute such an integrating center, though there is no attempt in Polanyi to develop a full theory of consciousness or personality in the psychological or psychiatric sense.

The rejection of Köhler's form of isomorphism is rooted in all the prior analyses – constituting a form of phenomenology – of all the conscious performances and in the crucial distinction between focal and subsidiary awareness as well as the ultimately tacit character of consciousness considered as *subjective experience*. Following the parts-whole model through to the end produced for Polanyi a conclusion radically different from that found in classical Gestalt theory. It made possible both a radical, autonomous examination of conscious, intentional performances – which Gestalt theory also wanted to do, albeit in truncated form – and the rejection of monism – which in the last analysis Gestalt theory wanted to affirm.

V. *Conclusion*

Gestalt theory furnished clues to Polanyi for an independent expansion of a general theory of knowledge and mind. Rather than concentrating fundamentally upon perception, as classical Gestalt theory did, Polanyi wanted to "establish an alternative ideal of knowledge, quite generally" (PK vii). The path to this conceptual reform was through countenancing the "philosophic implications of Gestalt," which were not known to Gestalt theory itself. Indeed, Polanyi had no intention of merely duplicating the accepted empirical analyses and findings of Gestalt theory but wanted to institute a total reflective exploration of the varieties of cognitive performances and their conditions.

His taking up of the structural analogy between knowledge and skill led him to discover the "personal coefficient" of all knowing, from cases of skilful motoric action to the appreciation of probability and order in the exact sciences. It further led him, by means of the reflection upon skills and the logic of parts and wholes, to the crucial distinction between focal and subsidiary awareness, which was missing in classical Gestalt theory. But Polanyi had no intention of simply applying, in rough and ready fashion, these notions to the data of cognitional process. His model of knowing is not fully appreciated if one does not attend to the vast realm of concrete analyses and examples in his work, only a minor portion of which could be brought forward in this paper.

In fact, what we have in Polanyi's work is a "phenomenology of science and knowledge"[24] whose aim is to articulate "the mental experiences of the subject" which consist in "an irreducible residue of mental operations."[25] While Polanyi's debt to Gestalt theory is real, it is by no means the only critical key to his work and references to Gestalt are found alongside equally important references to Piaget, Poincaré, Polya, Hadamard, and a veritable host of others. The greatest strength of Polanyi's epistemology is its constant closeness to actual cognitional processes, to authentic cognitive performances and achievements. Such a closeness is in keeping with the practical nature of Polanyi's enterprise: to familiarize ourselves with ourselves and our own mental faculties. Thus, Polanyi's concern is a form of self-appropriation, a taking possession of ourselves, by grasping the essential outlines of ourselves as knowers.

What we find in Polanyi's work is a set of clues which we have to integrate into an intelligible and comprehensive unity. This process involves a long set of integrations of subsidiarily intended particulars, Polanyi's own examples and analyses, from which we attend as we strive to grasp their joint meaning. That joint meaning is ourselves and our powers of intentional synthesis. The structure uncovered by our reflective appropriation of Polanyi's model of knowing is exemplified in the very processes we use to uncover it. Polanyi's project points to the self-engagement of the knower not just in knowing the world, but in knowing knowing itself.

Notes

1. See Steve Fuller, *Social Epistemology* (Bloomington: Indiana University Press, 1988) and Joseph Rouse, *Knowledge and Power: Toward a Political Philosophy of Science* (Ithaca: Cornell University Press, 1987) for stimulating discussions and introduction to the vast literature on the topic.
2. I will concentrate on the work of Wolfgang Köhler in this paper, since he plays the predominant role in Polanyi's own thought. There are references, however, to other figures in the Gestalt school such as Koffka and Wertheimer, but they are generally mentioned passant. Certain Gestalt biologists figure in Part IV of *Personal Knowledge*, but an extensive discussion of these topics is not possible in the present context. Koffka's large book, *Principles of Gestalt Psychology*, is a classic summation of experimental work up to 1935, but since Polanyi's reform of Gestalt theory was conceptual rather than empirical I did not think it worthwhile to burden the text with extensive references to fundamentally identical positions. References to Köhler's works will appear in abbreviated form in the body of the text according to the following rubrics: GP=*Gestalt Psychology* (New York: New American Library, 1959 [paper reissue of 1949 edition]), VWF=*The Place of Values in a World of Facts* (New York: Liveright, 1938), DP=*Dynamics in Psychology* (New York: Liveright, 1940). Other references will be cited according to standard practice. From the enormous secondary literature on Gestalt theory I would like to mention two in particular which are extremely useful for the philosopher: Paul Guillaume, *La Psychologie de la forme* (Paris: Flammarion, 1979 reprint) and Gaetano Kanizsa, *Grammatica del vedere* (Bologna: Il Mulino, 1980).
3. See my series of papers: 'Polanyi's Model of Mental Acts,' *The New Scholasticism* 47, 2, 1973, pp. 147-178, 'The Logic of Consciousness and the Mind-Body Problem in Polanyi,' *International Philosophical Quarterly* 13, 1, 1973, pp. 81-98, 'Meaning, Thought, and Language in Polanyi's Epistemology,' *Philosophy Today* 18, 1, 1974, pp. 47-67, 'The Triadic Structure of Religious Consciousness in Polanyi,' *The Thomist* 40, 3, 1976, pp. 393-415, 'Art, Symbol, Consciousness,' *International Philosophical Quarterly* 17, 4, 1977, pp. 455-476, and 'In Memoriam Michael Polanyi,' *Zeitschrift für allgemeine Wissenschaftstheorie* 8, 1, 1977, pp. 22-29. See also the stimulating book by Marjorie Grene, *The Knower and the Known* (Berkeley: University of California Press, 1974 [paper reissue]).
4. References to the major works of Polanyi will appear in abbreviated form in the body of the

text according to the following rubrics: SFS=*Science, Faith and Society* (Chicago: University of Chicago Press, 1964 [paper reissue]); LL=*The Logic of Liberty* (Chicago: University of Chicago Press, 1951); PK=*Personal Knowledge* (London: Routledge and Kegan Paul, 1958); SM=*The Study of Man* (Chicago: University of Chicago Press, 1958); TD=*The Tacit Dimension* (Garden City: Doubleday, 1967); M=*Meaning* (Chicago: University of Chicago Press, 1975). References to the essays collected in *Knowing and Being*, ed. Marjorie Grene (Chicago: University of Chicago Press, 1969) will be cited according to standard practice so as to specify the title of the particular essay being referred to, although KB will be used to cite the book.

5. See my paper, 'Heidegger's Model of Subjectivity: A Polanyian Critique', in Thomas Sheehan (ed.), *Heidegger, The Man and the Thinker* (Chicago: Precedent Press, 1981), pp. 117-130, where I have tried to draw out the parallels in their two projects.
6. See the index of PK for extensive references to maxims. This theme obviously has importance for moral and ethical theory in the Aristotelian mode, but I cannot go into that now.
7. George Polya, *How to Solve It* (Garden City: Doubleday, 1957).
8. Gerald Holton, *Thematic Origins of Scientific Thought* (Cambridge, MA: Harvard University Press, 1973). This volume has rich and illuminating studies that intersect with many of Polanyi's themes.
9. See the two books by Bernard Lonergan, *Verbum: Word and Idea in Aquinas*, edited by David B. Burrell (Notre Dame: University of Notre Dame Press, 1967), originally published as a series of articles in *Theological Studies* from 1946 through 1949 and his masterwork of systematic cognitional theory, *Insight* (London: Longmans, 1957), later reprinted in paperback by Harper's.
10. Among the many parallels and complements I would like to mention only the classic account of the 'pattern of inquiry,' in John Dewey, *Logic: The Theory of Inquiry* (New York: Henry Holt, 1938) and the discussions found in the well-known work of Norwood Russell Hanson, *Perception and Discovery* (San Francisco: Freeman, Cooper, and Co., 1969), Ludwig Fleck, *Genesis and Structure of a Scientific Fact*, translated by Fred Branley and Thaddeus J. Trenn, edited by Thaddeus J. Trenn and Robert K. Merton (Chicago: University of Chicago Press, 1979), Ludwig Fleck, *Erfahrung und Tatsache*, edited and introduced by Lothar Schäfer and Thomas Schnelle (Frankfurt: Suhrkamp, 1983), Thomas Kuhn's still relevant, *The Structure of Scientific Revolutions* (Chicago: University of Chicago Press, 1970 [second enlarged edition]), and Patrick Heelan, *Space-Perception and the Philosophy of Science* (Berkeley: University of California Press, 1983).
11. 'Tacit Knowing: Its Bearing on Some Problems of Philosophy,' in KB 160.
12. 'The Logic of Tacit Inference,' in KB 145.
13. 'Sense-Giving and Sense-Reading,' in KB 181.
14. See James Bunn, *The Dimensionality of Signs, Tools, and Models* (Bloomington: Indiana University Press, 1981).
15. See especially the massive and provocative work of George Lakoff, *Women, Fire, and Dangerous Things* (Chicago: University of Chicago Press, 1987) and the extensive literature cited there.
16. In this Polanyi relies upon and parallels the work of E. Sapir. See Sapir's great book *Language* (New York: Harcourt, Brace, and World, 1921) and his magnificent article 'Language' from *Encyclopedia of the Social Sciences* (New York: Macmillan, 1933), vol. 9, pp. 155-169, reprinted in E. Sapir, *Culture, Language, and Personality*, edited by David Mandelbaum (Berkeley: University of California Press, 1970).
17. In Mary Henle (ed.), *Documents of Gestalt Psychology* (Berkeley: University of California

Press, 1961), p. 75.
18. 'Life's Irreducible Structure,' KB 238.
19. *Ibid.*
20. *Ibid.*
21. 'The Structure of Consciousness,' KB 222.
22. *Ibid.*
23. *Ibid.*
24. 'The Logic of Tacit Inference," KB 155.
25. 'On Body and Mind,' *The New Scholasticism* 43 (1969), p. 202.

Danish Yearbook of Philosophy, Vol. **27** (1992), 45-71

THE PERCEPTUAL PARADIGM OF MORAL EPISTEMOLOGY

PETER SANDØE
University of Copenhagen

I. *Moral Knowledge, Common Sense, and the Perceptual Paradigm*

Is there any such thing as moral knowledge? Do we, for example, sometimes have knowledge about whether an action is unkind or disloyal to someone; or about whether something is morally right or wrong? In a sense these questions can only be answered with a clear 'yes' – except maybe by someone who has lost faith in morality altogether and is unable to take a moral stance.

However, there is a way to understand these questions, with a special emphasis on the word '*knowledge*', such that a negative answer does not have to be seen as an expression of failing moral commitment. Thus understood the questions are about whether some moral commitments or 'beliefs' can ever be epistemically superior to other competing commitments or 'beliefs'. Epistemic superiority implies, at least, that there is something in virtue of which the relevant view is superior, over and above the fact that we or some other human beings hold, or feel attached to, the view. And a negative answer might be based on doubts as to whether there is anything which is sufficient to make some moral judgments superior in this way.

Most 'ordinary' people in our modern, secular world would, I think, be inclined to give a negative answer to the questions understood in this latter way. They are sceptical about the existence of moral knowledge; their scepticism could be compared with the scepticism that nearly all of us feel concerning ghosts: we don't believe that there are any such entities.

I am aware that not all philosophers agree with me when I say that ordinary people are sceptical about moral knowledge. Let me therefore, briefly outline the sort of experiences on which I base this claim, and explain in a little more detail the sort of scepticism I have in mind.

By 'ordinary people' I here mean persons who know nothing, or virtually nothing, about what philosophers, and specifically analytical philosophers, say about morality. My own experience, however, is of persons from one small corner of the world only, and mainly from one section of the population. They are Danish people whom I have taught in evening classes on moral philosophy and people I have met on more informal social occasions. I cannot therefore claim that the views I am going to present are representative of 'ordinary people' in general, though I do think they are at least representative of modern middle class Western Europeans of the sort who, like most Danes, do not have any firm religious convictions.

When these people are presented with the idea that there could be moral facts, or canons of moral rationality, in virtue of which it could be said to be morally right, or morally wrong, or the like, for us to do or not to do certain things, their reaction is sceptical. When asked why they think that there are no such facts or canons of rationality, which allow us to say that some actions are simply morally right and others morally wrong, irrespective of what we actually think is right or wrong, they reply by pointing to the great divergence of actual moral views. They point out that what is morally right or wrong differs from age to age, from society to society, from class to class and so on.

Sometimes, I have then confronted such people with the simple text-book argument against concluding, on the basis of the observation that moral practices differ, that these different practices reflect conflicting moralities: the different practices could just as well be seen as the same basic moral outlook applied to different circumstances or different views about the world. Secondly, I have pointed out that if different or conflicting moral views across cultures and ages were a reason for not believing in moral objectivity there would be a similar reason for saying that there is no objectivity in science.

To this the typical response is to say that there is a crucial difference here between science and morality in that science has means by which it can find and test hypotheses about nature, whereas we have no way of testing our moral views. So although it may be right that we agree about how to answer many moral questions there is no way we can certify that what we agree about is true. In other words, if someone came along who had moral views different from ours there would be no way we could prove him wrong.

At this stage of the dialogue I have sometimes called attention to the fact that scientists disagree strongly over matters which are dealt with by the sciences. For example, there is no consensus over whether quantum mechanics gives us a true picture of physical reality, even though this question has been discussed by leading scientists for more than four decades. To this observation those of my interlocutors who have not insisted on changing the subject have responded by saying that at least we have an idea of what it would be for the physicists to find out what is the right account of physical reality, whereas we have no similar idea in the case of morality.

What is noteworthy about the view of the 'ordinary' man as here developed is that it is epistemological and not primarily ontological in nature. The question is not, 'How could there be a moral reality?', but rather, 'How could we, even in ideal circumstances, know about moral facts?'. The basic assumption underlying common sense scepticism about morality is not one about the existence or non-existence of physical and moral facts or other entities. It is an assumption about the difference between the best possible physical theory (or any other basic scientific theory) and the best possible moral outlook, where both science and morality are taken to share important features with science and morality as *we* know them. The last clause is very important. If it is not there, then the assumption that the best possible physical theory tells us what the world is like is no longer interestingly different from the ontological assumption that the world contains physical facts (whatever they might be).

Scepticism about moral knowledge of the sort just outlined is a view that is also shared by many modern philosophers. It became prominent in the first half of this century, mainly through the influence of logical positivism. However, the view has come loose from its positivist underpinnings, such as the principles of verification or falsification, and the claim that there is an exclusive distinction between descriptive and evaluative judgments, etc. Part of the explanation for this seems to be that even though philosophers no longer think they have a clear criterion by which they can demarcate propositions that are cognitively meaningful from those which are not, many philosophers still think that the line of demarcation should be drawn where all the proposed criteria intended to draw it: that is between propositions which can be tested or otherwise challenged by the methods of science and those which cannot.[1] Of course, we still don't know what science is; but we are pretty confident that answers to our moral questions are not to be found by scientific methods. And since moral judgments cannot be integrated into modern science they cannot express knowledge.

Even though this may be a good explanation of why many people endorse a sceptical attitude towards the existence of moral knowledge, it is surely not a very good argument. It relies on the highly dubious premise that only judgments which can be integrated into modern science can express knowledge. Are there better arguments to be found, or is the widespread scepticism about the existence of moral knowledge just an indication that most of us yield to some sort of scientism? In this paper I shall consider a view according to which scepticism concerning moral knowlegde is not well founded.

This view is based on a set of ideas which I shall call *the perceptual paradigm of moral epistemology*. The most consistent version of this paradigm is found in the writings of John McDowell.[2] My prime aim is not to give an exegesis of McDowell's views. Rather, I take some of his ideas, particularly his account of the analogy between values and secondary qualities, as my starting point and try to find out to what extent they can be sustained.

The following quotation from McDowell may give the gist of these ideas, and also explain why I have chosen to call the account of moral knowledge based on these ideas the perceptual paradigm of moral epistemology:

> A kind person can be relied on to behave kindly when that is what the situation requires. Moreover, his reliably kind behaviour is not the outcome of a blind, non-rational habit or instinct, like the courageous behaviour – so called only by courtesy – of a lioness defending her cubs. Rather, that the situation requires a certain sort of behaviour is (one way of formulating) his reason for behaving in that way, on each of the relevant occasions. So it must be something of which, on each of the relevant occasions, he is aware. A kind person has a reliable sensitivity to a certain sort of requirement which situations impose on behaviour. The deliverances of a reliable sensitivity are cases of knowledge; and there are idioms according to which the sensitivity itself can appropriately be described as knowledge: a kind person knows what it is like to be confronted with a requirement of kindness. The sensitivity is, we might say, a sort of perceptual capacity.[3]

The key idea – suggested by Aristotle's use of the idea of aisthesis – is that when a situation evokes a moral attitude in us, this attitude itself can be the result of a genuine awareness of a moral quality of the situation. Our attitudes inform us about moral features of the world in a way analogous to the way in which ordinary sense impressions inform us about the sounds, colours, shapes and other sensory properties of the objects surrounding us.[4]

This idea, of course, needs a lot of elaboration and clarification, which I shall try to provide in the following sections. But first I would like to say a little about what in the first instance motivates a perceptual account of moral epistemology.

A perceptual account is allegedly in accordance with how moral thought presents itself. Thus according to McDowell:

> The phenomenology of value experience in general suggests a visual model for our dealing with value.[5]

Of course, this gives at most a *prima facie* reason for accepting the perceptual paradigm. Even if the phenomenological claim gives a correct account of our ordinary moral thinking, our moral thinking may still be presenting itself in a wrong way.[6]

And I think that it is possible to doubt the correctness of McDowell's description of how ordinary moral thought presents itself. It is true that moral thought appears to be about something objective, something that we have to find out rather than invent or freely decide. But this fact does not tell in favour, particularly, of a perceptual or even a realist model of moral thought.[7]

A constructivist model of moral thinking like the one favoured by Kant or the one found in R.M. Hare's recent work will, as far as I can see, do just as much justice to the phenomenology as does McDowell's perceptual model. According to the constructivist model moral judgments are imperatives or prescriptions governed by requirements of rationality. These requirements may, in conjunction with relevant information about the world, determine correct answers to our moral questions. And this will allow moral thought to be about something objective, something which we have to find out rather than invent.[8]

So the argument from phenomenology is less than compelling. Furthermore, there seems to be a clear tension between the phenomenological claim as I have just interpreted it and the claim, argued for in the beginning of this section, that ordinary people are sceptical about the existence of moral knowledge. If the latter claim is true, will that not completely undermine the phenomenological claim?

Not quite, I think. The tension between the two claims is in more than one sense a very real one. Even though ordinary people officially do not believe that there is any moral knowledge to be found, they still often conduct their moral thinking as if there were. They engage in heavy moral thinking, argue about their moral views, and often claim about others that they fail to see what is obviously true. So in a sense ordinary people seem to be in two minds about the existence of moral knowledge. And therefore the official scepticism about moral knowledge will not refute the phenomenological claim. At most it will weaken its force as a reason in favour of ethical objectivity.

The phenomenological thesis as McDowell interprets it is not primarily a claim to the effect that our moral thoughts seem to contain knowledge, but is rather a claim concerning what our moral thoughts appear to be thoughts *about*. McDowell claims that moral thoughts seem to be about the world:

> ... ordinary evaluative thought presents itself as a matter of sensitivity to aspects of the world. An this phemenological thesis seems correct.[9]

If our self-understanding is as McDowell here says it is, and if we are right in understanding ourselves in this way, what follows is something *about the world*. This might be spelled out by saying that there are moral facts, or by saying that moral qualities are real properties of the things or actions to which they are ascribed. The phenomenology seems to support some sort of *moral realism*.

II. *Modest Moral Realism and the Analogy between Values and Secondary Qualities*

Jonn McDowell and other adherents of the perceptual paradigm of moral epistemology claim that things and actions really have moral qualities of the sorts which we ascribe to them in our moral judgments. The kind of moral realism entailed by this claim, however, differs importantly from the two competing realist views which, in traditional textbooks on ethical theory, are presented as together occupying the whole possible territory of realist positions.[10] The two views, which are usually called *intuitionism* and *naturalism*, disagree over whether evaluative properties can be reduced to other sorts of properties, notably 'natural' ones, and over whether evaluative properties are known by the same or similar means as those by which we get to know empirical facts. But they share an important feature which is brought out in a standard argument against these views made by adherents of prescriptivism, emotivism and similar views.

This is the argument which bases itself on the claim that, if one sincerely evaluates a certain thing or action in a certain way, one is thereby bound to be *motivated* in a certain appropriate way. For example, if one sincerely says that it is morally wrong for husbands to beat their wives, one is thereby bound to be repelled by such actions, or to think that men should abstain from them. And, so the argument goes, this is something which naturalists and intuitionists are not able to account for, since, on their view, to evaluate a thing or an action in a certain way is simply to ascribe a property to it which it is thought to have quite independently of our attitudes and propensities to act.[11]

A realist view will, of course, only be vulnerable to this argument if it assumes that the properties we ascribe to things and actions are ones which things and actions are thought to have independently of our attitudes and propensities to act. But this assumption is explicitly denied by the kind of realist view that I shall consider here. The basic idea which makes this denial tenable is expressed by John McDowell in the following way:

> ... we can learn to see the world in terms of some specific set of evaluative classifications, aesthetic or moral, only because our affective and attitudinative propensities are such that we can be brought to care in appropriate ways about the things we learn to see as collected together by the classifications.[12]

The idea is that evaluative properties can only be apprehended because we have certain attitudes towards the things and actions which have those evaluative properties. Evaluative properties are, so to speak, experienced in the light of the relevant attitudes. And therefore the adherent of this sort of realism, *modest realism* as I shall call it, has no problem explaining why sincerely ascribing an evaluative property to a thing or an action is necessarily accompanied by a certain attitude towards the thing or action.

A first reaction by traditionally minded philosophers towards modest realism will probably be to say that it isn't a version of realism at all. Their reason for saying so might run something like this. For a property to be a 'real' property it must be one which the object to which it is truly ascribed would have had even if we who ascribe it had other attitudes, emotions and other subjective propensities than those we actually have. The claim made by 'modest realism', that evaluative properties can only be singled out because we have the subjective propensities we actually have, entails that, if we had different propensities then the objects to which we ascribe evaluative properties would not have the evaluative properties they presently have. And from these two premises the conclusion follows that evaluative properties as conceived by 'modest realism' cannot be real.

On the face of it this appears a very forceful argument. However, the modest moral realist has a way of answering it. The answer[13] grants the condition for objectivity set up in the argument's first premise but denies the second premise. More specifically, it is the general metaphysical principle underlying the second premise that is rejected, viz. the principle that if a property is subjective then it must also be relative. The adherent of modest realism claims that a property can be subjective in the sense that for a thing to have the property is for it to be disposed to elicit a certain subjective response, without it being true that the objects which actually have these properties would not have had them had we had other subjective propensities than those we actually have. This is, of course, a claim that must be argued for. And the best way to do this seems to be by exploiting a parallel with secondary qualities.

In the rest of this paper I shall discuss the analogy between values and secondary qualities used as a defence of the perceptual paradigm of moral epistemology.[14] This use of the analogy relies on two premises, both of which are highly controversial. The first is that secondary qualities are both subjective and objective in the relevant respects. The second premise is that moral values are sufficiently like secondary qualities for the analogy to go through. The first premise I have defended elsewhere[15], and I shall therefore here concentrate on the second one.

III. *Absolutist Dispositional Accounts of Moral Values*

I shall assume, at least for the sake of argument, that secondary qualities are both subjective and intrinsic. To model an account of moral values on secondary qualities one should, therefore, claim that moral values are subjective in the sense that, what it is for a thing or an action to possess a certain sort of moral value, cannot be specified without reference to how, in certain circumstances, we would respond to the thing. And one should say that values are also objective in the sense that value properties are intrinsic properties of the things or actions to which they are (truly) ascribed – properties which cannot change unless their bearers undergo a real change.

The claim that moral values are subjective has been very influential in modern philosophy; first person subjectivist naturalists[16] and emotivists alike have argued that moral judgments are to be analysed in terms of the attitudes or emotions evoked in us by the things to which we ascribe value. However, it has generally been thought to be a consequence of such views that moral values cannot be objective in the required sense. Either things and actions simply do not have value-properties (if emotivism is true), or else such properties are straightforwardly relative[17] (if subjectivist naturalism is true). According to a first person subjectivist, for an action to be morally wrong is for it to evoke a certain feeling of disapproval *in me*. But since an action that evokes such a feeling might conceivably evoke the opposite feeling in another person, the same action which is morally wrong (to me) might be morally right (to the other person).

So it has generally been thought that the claim that moral values are subjective entails, either that things do not have value properties, or that such properties are relative. However, some philosophers have seen that there is a third possibility, namely that moral values could at the same time be subjective and objective . Examples apart from the two already mentioned, i.e. John McDowell and David Wiggins, are C.D. Broad[18] 18 and Roderick Firth.

In a famous paper Firth suggests the possibility of giving what he calls an 'absolutist dispositional' analysis of ethical statements – meaning by 'absolutist' roughly what I mean by 'objective' and by 'dispositional' what I mean by 'subjective'. Firth tries to make such an account seem credible by comparing values with secondary qualities.
He writes:

> ... if an absolutist dispositional analysis were correct, ethical statements would have the same form that statements about secondary qualities are often supposed to have. ... to say that a daffodil is yellow is to say something about the way the daffodil would appear to a certain kind of observer under certain conditions; and the analysis of ethical statements which we are considering is exactly analogous to this.[19]

It may be an exaggeration to say that the account of ethical statements that Firth goes on to elaborate is '*exactly* analogous' to a dispositional account of secondary qualities. The kind of 'ideal' observer by reference to which he analyses what it is for a thing or an action to have certain moral properties is distinguished by, among other things, intellectual qualities such as omniscience and omnipercipience, which are irrelevant to the perception of secondary qualities.[20] To mirror these qualities in us intellectual activities are called for in a way that will make the process by which we find out about the moral qualities of things and actions quite different from the direct and immediate way in which we normally perceive secondary qualities.

I think something like this is what underlies the following "crucial disanalogy" between values and secondary qualities noted by John McDowell:

> The disanalogy ... is that a virtue (say) is conceived to be not merely such as to elicit the appropriate 'attitude' (as a colour is merely such as to cause the appropriate experiences), but rather such as to *merit* it.[21]

McDowell's point, I take it, is not to reject a perceptual model for our knowledge of moral qualities. Rather, it is to emphasize that to be able to get a clear view of the moral qualities of a thing or an action we may have to go through processes of a more intellectual kind than those involved in perception of secondary qualities. For a thing or an action to have a certain moral property is for it to be disposed to evoke a certain response in us, when properly situated. And to be reasonably confident that we are in the right frame of mind to perceive the quality a great deal of reflection may be necessary.[22]

Thus according to McDowell:

> ... ethical reality is immensely difficult to see clearly.
> ... If we are aware how, for instance, selfish fantasy distorts our vision, we shall not be inclined to be confident that we have got things right.[23]

It is hard to specify what it takes for us to become ideal moral observers. Firth's specific account has been widely criticized, but very few of the critics have considered the merits of Firth's general approach, in spite of the fact that Firth is himself very concerned to make clear that the general approach does not stand or fall with his specific version of the theory; "it would", he says "be especially unfortunate if the inadequacies of some particular formulation were to prejudice philosophers against absolutist dispositional analyses in general".[24]

R.B. Brandt, however, notices the merits of the general approach. At the beginning of a discussion of Firth's theory he mentions seven, of which I shall here quote five:

> (1) that this theory enables us to regard as really relevant to ethics all the facts which on reflection we take to be relevant; (2) that it enables us to explain the heterogeneousness of the actions which we regard as right or wrong; (3) that it explains how ethical disagreement is possible even when there is agreement about the nature of the act being appraised; (4) that it explains why our feelings and attitudes – and especially our sympathies – are (and properly are) engaged in ethical reflection, and why moral philosophers have thought that moral experience is distinctively a union of cognition and emotion; (5) that it enables us to hold that moral opinions are subject to objective criticism and are correct or incorrect ... [25]

The first of the alleged merits is of a very general nature, and it would probably not impress someone who was in doubt about the whole approach. The next four, however, do point to obvious, *prima facie*, advantages of the theory over some of its major competitors. Let me try to spell this out in a little more detail.

(2) shows the advantage of the theory over theories which claim that things or actions sharing a certain moral property have something in common that we can make sense of quite independently of the sort of interest we take in those things or actions. G.E. Moore's account of goodness as a simple property is one such theory; and it is notoriously difficult to 'see' any one such property shared by good things, or even by the few things that Moore claims are intrinsically good, i.e. enjoyment of beautiful things, friendship and love.[26]

(3) marks an advantage of the theory over first person subjectivism and emotivism. According to subjectivism two persons cannot genuinely disagree in their respective moral judgments, since each, in making a moral judgment, is talking only about his own reaction to the thing or action in question.[27] And according to emotivism there is no such thing as genuine ethical disagreement – what looks like ethical disagreement is either disagreement about factual matters, or sounding offs of 'conflicting' emotions. Of course, it is a matter of debate whether first person subjectivists and emotivists could not explain apparent moral disagreements in terms of factual disagreement and/or 'conflicting' emotions.[28] However, it is a *prima facie* advantage of a dispositional theory that it allows basic ethical disagreement to be a genuine sort of disagreement, for example disagreement over how a properly situated moral agent would respond to a thing or an action of the sort in question.

(4) marks a clear advantage over traditional versions of moral realism, both of naturalistic and intuitionistic sorts. It is now widely agreed that moral values are linked to human feelings and attitudes: to 'see' that an action has a certain moral quality is, in a typical case, to be emotionally involved with the fact (or the possible fact) that the action is, or is not, being done.[29] Some naturalists have tried to explain this by claiming that moral properties are linked to things which we care about anyway for prudential reasons, but they have not been notably successful.[30] On the dispositional view, by contrast, it is not difficult to explain why our emotions are involved in finding out the moral properties of things or actions.[31]

Finally, (5) points to an advantage of the dispositional view over certain sorts of moral realism which have difficulties in explaining how it is possible to engage in criticism of other people's moral views. On some versions of ethical intuitionism it is difficult to explain how I can criticize another person's moral views except by simply stating that they are wrong.[32] On the dispositional view, by contrast, it is possible to criticize a person's moral judgments, for example, by pointing out that he was in the wrong frame of mind or was viewinq the situation from a wrong perspective when he made his judgments.

So it seems that a dispositional account of moral values has a number of advantages over some of its prominent competitors. That these advantages are not outweighed by shortcomings of other sorts, of course, remains to be seen.

In the rest of the paper I shall discuss two alleged shortcomings of dispositional accounts of moral value. The first, to be dealt with in the next section, is that dispositional accounts are circular. The other, which I shall discuss in the last section of the paper, is that it is not possible to account for moral 'blindness' by analogy with colour blindness.

IV. *Is a Dispositional Account of Moral Value Bound to End in a Vicious Circle?*

It may be argued that a dispositional theory of moral value, despite its apparent advantages, cannot really explain what it is supposed to explain. Thus Gilbert Harman claims that a dispositional theory cannot specify in a non-circular way the sort of human response by reference to which the theory aims to analyze what it is for an action to have a moral property, say, the property of being morally wrong:

> ... what sort of disapproval is it that the ideal observer has to feel in order for something to be wrong? To say, simply, 'disapproval' is inadequate. The ideal observer might, for example, feel aesthetic disapproval without there being anything morally wrong. If Oswald does a dance that an ideal observer would disapprove of on purely aesthetic grounds, Oswald has not yet done anything morally wrong. But, if we say 'moral disapproval,' what does that come to over and above 'the judgment that something is wrong?' To define 'X is wrong' as 'an ideal observer would feel moral disapproval of X' is very much like defining 'X is wrong' as 'an ideal observer would think that X is wrong.' And that would be circular; we would be using the term 'wrong' to analyze the term 'wrong'.[33]

The first thing to be noted about this argument is that, if it works, there will be an equally devastating argument against a dispositional account of secondary qualities. On such an account what it is for a thing to have a certain secondary quality can only be explained by reference to a certain sort of subjective sense-experience; for a thing to be yellow for example is for it to *look yellow* to a certain sort of perceiver in certain circumstances. But here too, so the analogous argument would go, the very term to be explained, 'yellow', is used in the explanation itself.[34]

There seem to be two ways of dealing with this argument. The first is to claim that the terms to be explained, e.g. 'wrong' and 'yellow', are not really used in the relevant explanations. The expressions used are 'feeling wrong' and 'looking yellow', and these expressions are treated as primitives denoting different sorts of 'simple' subjective states, 'qualia', know by introspection. This answer is sufficient to block the argument, but it gives rise to a number of acute problems.

First, on this view it must be admitted as a possibility that different people when presented with the same things might have widely different subjective states without there being any chance of finding out that this is the case. When confronted with things that look yellow to me other people might be presented with the same qualia that I am presented with when I look at red things, and so on, for the other colours. But in this case there will be no one colour that a daffodil has; either it will have no colour at all, or it will have colours in a relativized sense according to which it is yellow to me and (say) red to another person. However, since there would be no way in which this could be detected (assuming we make equally fine colour discriminations) there would be no way in which it could be found out that there was such a difference.

The other person and I would, in a perfectly ordinary sense of 'communicate', have no problems whatsoever in communicating about the colours of things. For example, if I tell him that my house has been painted yellow, he will perfectly well know what to expect to see next time he comes to visit me in my house. So, it seems that when we use the word 'yellow' to communicate with each other we actually understand the same thing by the word. However, this same thing is not accounted for by the analysis of the quality yellow referring to an unanalysable subjective quale of yellowness. So, apart from the well-known difficulties about accounting for the existence of qualia,[35] this sort of analysis is not able to give a full account of our actual use of colour words.

This line of argument, of course, just echoes well-known points made by Wittgenstein in *Philosophical Investigations* more than three decades ago. And since these points do not enjoy general acceptance among philosophers I am under no illusion that my argument will convince those who think that colours should be analysed by reference to qualia.

The other and, I think, more promising way to deal with Harman's argument, which has been suggested by David Wigins,[36] is to admit the conclusion and then argue that it is not fatal to the types of account of values and secondary qualities under consideration here. The conclusion of Harman's argument is only problematic to the extent that those accounts are supposed to be *analyses*. For, in a proper analysis the analysans should be intelligible to someone who does not have a prior grasp of the analysandum. But maybe it is too much to ask of an explanation that it be an analysis in this sense. The following simple example from another area of philosophy suggests this.

Suppose someone wants me to give him an explanation of what a sentence is. I go on tell him that a sentence is something that is essentially composed of parts; for example a simple sentence can be composed of a name and a predicate. Of course, I admit to him, I have not here given an exhaustive explanation of what a sentence is; but it seems that I have given at least a reasonable explanation of what a sentence can be. Imagine though that he goes on to ask *what* a predicate is. I present him with a number of examples of predicates, '... is red', '...is a cow', '... is made in Denmark', '... is taller than ' and so on; and I invite him to give me examples, and I correct him, until I am reasonably confident that he knows a predicate when he sees it. Assume, however, that he, under the influence perhaps of Plato or G.E. Moore, complains that though he knows how to distinguish predicates from other linguistic entities, he still does not know what a predicate is. I then tell him that a predicate is something that combined in the right way with a name becomes a simple sentence. But this will not satisfy him; quite to the contrary, since I am using the concept 'sentence' to define the concept in terms of which I was analysing the very concept sentence, the attempt to give an analysis of what a sentence is has, he would say, broken down. We are no wiser than we were at the outset.

If he then asked me to provide a better analysis of what a sentence is, I could offer an explanation in terms of concepts like 'truth', 'assertion', 'thought', or 'communication'. But I should warn him that in the end, if he pressed me to explain those concepts too, I would have to rely on the very concept of a sentence as a part of that explanation.

Would this really allow him to say that it is impossible to give an informative explanation of what a sentence is? No, as far as I can see the suggested explanations of what a sentence is are as informative as they can be.[37]

So the suggestion is that it is not necessary for the adherent of a dispositional account of some quality Q to require that the subjective responses, by reference to which it is explained what it is for a thing to have the quality Q, should be intelligible independently of any prior knowledge of what it is for a thing to have the quality Q. Even if the account does not satisfy this requirement it can give an explanation which is as informative as one should expect such an explanation to be.

An adherent of the dispositional view of moral values who does not claim to provide analyses can explain what it is for a thing or an action to have a certain kind of value V in a number of ways. He can first point out a fair sample of things or actions which have the quality V; he can supplement this by pointing out features of the things or actions in question which are particularly relevant to their being V; he can then go on to say something more specific about the kind of attitude in virtue of which we become aware of a thing being V – how it is linked up with propensities to act in certain ways, for example. Finally he can go on to say something about the state of mind one must be in for one's attitudes to be a reliable detector of the V-ness of things or actions.

As for the specific problem alluded to by Harman in the quotation given above of how to distinguish on a dispositional account between aesthetic and moral 'wrongness', there seem to be a number of possible replies. For example it can be noted that moral wrongness attaches to actions which affect the wants and interests of more than one person, and that aesthetic wrongness is something that is not necessarily to be blamed.

The important thing to notice is that as long as the ambition is not to explain moral or aesthetic qualities in terms of subjective reactions which are intelligible independently of the moral or aesthetic qualities themselves, there is nothing wrong about specifying the relevant subjective reactions partly by reference to the qualities and the circumstances under which they are properly ascribed.

This reply to Harman's argument will leave the adherent of the perceptual paradigm with a version of moral realism that is 'modest' in the following respect – a respect which was not noted in the above characterization of modest moral realism: A claim sometimes associated with the notion of moral realism is that moral qualities are conceptually prior to the responses on the basis of which these qualities are ascribed to things and actions. This claim the modest realist will reject; but he will also reject the opposite claim, associated with irrealism or anti-realism, that our moral responses are conceptually prior to the alleged moral qualities.[38] The adherent of the perceptual paradigm will occupy a middle ground between traditional moral realism and the opposing irrealist or anti-realist views.

V. *'Moral Blindness' and Colour Blindness*

According to a dispositional theory of moral value, modelled on the account of secondary qualities given in the previous chapter, for a thing or an action to have a certain moral value is for it to be disposed to evoke a certain emotional response in *us*. In the previous section I have argued that such a theory need not be viciously circular. However, it might be argued that even if the theory is not viciously circular it fails due to an indeterminacy: there is no *one* way in which all possible human beings will respond emotionally to the relevant things and actions. We can imagine human beings who, for example, would respond with glee to actions which fill us with moral indignation.

The quick reply to this argument is that what determines the moral quality of a thing or an action is not that it is disposed to evoke a certain response in any possible human being, but that it is disposed to evoke it in *us*, as we *actually* are. This reply is significantly similar to a reply that I have elsewhere[39] suggested to an influential argument against the objectivity of secondary qualities, the so-called Phenol Argument. According to this argument secondary qualities cannot be objective because we can imagine that future human beings might undergo genetic changes so that they will be disposed to make secondary quality classifications which are incompatible with ours. The reply was that for a thing to have a certain secondary quality is for it to be disposed to produce a certain sensory impression in us, as we *actually* are. And if human beings in the future change so that they no longer are like us in the relevant respect this does not imply that things change the secondary qualities that we perceive them as having, rather the future humans will no longer be able to perceive these qualities.

However, for these two replies to go through it must be assumed that, given ideal circumstances, there is one, and only one, set of ways in which 'we' are disposed to 'see' things and actions.

As far as secondary qualities are concerned these assumptions seem to hold good. In most cases, there is one, and only one, way in which we are disposed to classify the colours, sounds, smells and other secondary qualities of things.[40] And the exceptions can be dealt with within the dispositional theory. In those cases in which we do not all have the same experiences, as in the case of the taste of phenol-thio-urea, it is reasonable to say that the corresponding secondary quality predicates are not well-defined for the relevant cases. It may be said that there is in such a case no fact of the matter as to whether or not the thing or substance has the relevant secondary quality. In other cases there is qeneral agreement as to what it takes to be a 'normal' perceiver. For example, in the case of colour-blindness it is agreed by all, including the colour-blind themselves, that some of us, i.e. those who are able to make the finest colour-discriminations, are 'normal' perceivers and therefore have the authority to tell which colour things have.

Can the assumptions also be defended in the case of moral values? First of all, to say that 'we' all share the same basic moral outlook is simply not true, if by 'we' is meant, for example, all members of democratic societies of the Western world. And even if differences in moral views which stem from differences in non-moral beliefs are ignored, the claim is still not very plausible. Consider contentious moral issues like those concerning distributive justice, abortion, pacifism and vegetarianism. On such issues there seem to be deep-rooted differences about what is seen as morally right and wrong – differences which cannot simply be explained by reference to variations in non-moral beliefs, or to other sorts of circumstances which are less than ideal. So, at least, I shall, provisionally, allow myself to assume.

However, maybe such differences in moral views can be explained by saying that some of us suffer from a deficient ability to make moral discriminations, comparable to colour blindness. That this might be the case has been suggested by Gilbert Harman:

> Not all perceivers have the same color reactions under standard conditions, since some perceivers are colorblind. These perceivers can be classed as substandard because, first of all, their reactions are not as sensitive as those of normal perceivers (color-blind perceivers make fewer color discriminations) and, second, normal perceivers who are able to make the most discriminations do agree in their color reactions. What is true for color *might* turn out to be true for moral properties too. For it is *conceivable* that we can

> explain disagreements among apparently ideal moral observers by supposing that some otherwise ideal observers have a kind of moral blindness, resulting either from some sort of genetic defect or a failure in their upbringing – for example, not enough love in their earliest years. To make this claim stick it would have to be shown that this group of apparently ideal observers do not make all the moral discriminations that other ideal observers make, although the other observers make all the discriminations the first group make. Furthermore, it would have to be shown that the other ideal observers for the most part have the same moral reactions.
>
> It is not wildly implausible that something like this might be shown. Psychological studies of the moral development of children indicate that there are a number of stages to this development, stages of increasing sophistication. Not everyone reaches the final stages of development. We might want to define rightness and wrongness only in terms of the reactions of those who have reached the highest stage of moral development, treating others as possessing a kind of moral blindness or some other deficiency.[41]

There are, I think, two questions at issue in this suggestive passage, and they ought to be kept apart. The first concerns whether or not there is a moral equivalent of colour-blindness; and the second whether or not such 'moral blindness' can serve to account for all, or nearly all, substantial moral disagreements between us.

On Harman's view, for someone to be colour-blind he must see *less* than the rest of us do in a fairly literal sense. This shows itself in the fact that he sees as having the same colour things which we perceive as having different colours. It is not just that he *chooses* to lump together under one concept what the rest of us want to separate under two concepts, as for example some people lump apes and monkeys together under the concept 'monkey'. He is simply unable to distinguish colours which the rest of us see as clearly different.

It is not difficult to find analogies to this in people's abilities to 'see' moral properties. Some people are not able to see the difference between impertinence and straightforwardness; and others are not able to distinguish officiousness from being helpful to others. Typically such people will use at most one of the concepts of the pair, and when being asked whether they can't see the difference between, for example, a remark which we think is impertinent and one which we take to be straightforward they will answer simply that they cannot.

However, the notion of not being able to see a moral difference between two things or actions is somewhat more tricky than the notion of not being able to see a difference in colour between two things, for the former notion seems to run together two things in a way that the latter doesn't. Not being able to see a moral difference can mean either 'not seeing any difference which could form the basis of a moral distinction' or 'seeing the difference but not taking it to be morally significant'. In the case of colour vision no such distinction seems possible. If one sees a difference between two things which for some people would be a reason for saying that the two things have different colours, then one *eo ipso* sees a difference which (from a theoretical point of view, at least) is significant.

It might be argued that there is no moral equivalent of colour-blindness because all cases of 'moral blindness' are cases of seeing (or at least being able to see) the difference but not taking it to be morally significant. This, it might be claimed, is not a case of being unable to make 'perceptual' discriminations that other, so-called normal, people can make. Rather, it is a case of not taking the same attitudes to what one sees as other people do; we all see the same but just feel differently about it. So there is nothing to which the morally blind person is blind.

Thus stated the argument will probably not impress the adherent of the perceptual paradigm. For it seems to beg the question at issue. According to the paradigm as specified above moral properties are experienced in the light of one's attitudes; and if one hasn't got the relevant attitude then there is something that one doesn't see. And, it might be claimed, this is strictly analogous to colour vision. If one does not possess the capacity to obtain different colour experiences when being confronted with things of a different colour, then there is something in the world that one does not see, namely the relevant differences in colour. For the argument to have any force it must be shown that there is a clear sense in which the morally blind person does see the very same as a person with a normal moral outlook – a sense which is not analogous to any sense in which the colour-blind person can be said to see the same as what is seen by a person with a normal colour vision.

A proponent of the argument can at least present an account of the epistemology of morals according to which there *is* a sense in which the morally blind person sees the same as a person with a normal moral outlook. On this account what we are aware of, or think we are aware of, when we ascribe a moral property to a thing or an action is a set of non-moral properties. This set of non-moral properties constitutes *our reason* for ascribing the moral property; and what we do in ascribing the moral property is, so to speak, to add a moral extra to the non-moral properties we are aware of.

However, the modest realist might say that, since we are not usually able to distinguish two such elements in our moral judgments, there is no reason to believe in this two-component account of moral thinking. I shall here allow the modest realist the benefit of the doubt. And he may therefore assume that the two-component theory is, as McDowell puts it, "a prejudice, without intrinsic plausibility."[42]

So I assume for the sake of argument that the adherent of the perceptual paradigm is entitled to deny that there is a relevant sense in which the morally blind person sees the same as a person with a normal moral outlook – a sense which is unlike any sense in which the colour-blind person can be said to see the same as what is seen by a person with a normal colour vision. This does not, of course, force him to deny that there are important differences between colour vision and moral sensibility like the following one noted by Simon Blackburn:

> The receptive mechanisms whereby we are acquainted with secondary properties are wellknown objects of scientific study. For example, the kinds of damage to the retina or the ear or taste buds which result in defective perception of secondary qualities can be studied. These studies are not at all similar to studies of defects of character which lead to moral blindness: these latter studies have no receptive or causal mechanisms as their topic. This is just as well, for we need to put things in a particular moral light after we are told about their *other* properties; we do not *also* have to wheel a particular sensory mechanism up against them.[43]

However, the adherent of the perceptual paradigm will point out that 'putting things in a particular moral light' need not, and indeed should not, be interpreted so as to imply a 'two-component' account of moral knowledge. When one puts things in a particular moral light one carves up the world in a way that need not be codifiable in non-moral terms. Therefore even if the morally blind person is able to distinguish all the nonmoral differences between two things or actions, he need not be able to tell whether there are any differences between them of the sort which the normal moral observer will count as morally relevant. And this is so even if he has seen and been told on previous occasions how a normal observer uses the relevant moral words.

Even if there is a moral equivalent of colour-blindness, however, it does not immediately follow that all differences in our moral sensitivities can be explained away by saying that some people suffer from 'moral blindness'. Not all differences need be of such a kind that they can be accounted for in this way.

Thus Colin McGinn has argued that very few of them, if any at all, are of that kind. He agrees with Harman concerning the nature of colour-blindness:

> The deficiency of the colour-blind is basically a matter of making fewer or coarser colour discriminations that those made by normal perceivers ...[44]

But he does not think that it is possible to explain moral error in a similar way. His main argument runs as follows:

> ... superiority of moral judgement does not consist solely (if it consists at all) in the ability merely to make *more* discriminations than others; it consists in being *right* in one's judgements about particular cases. Two people could in principle be capable of making equally fine-grained moral distinctions, and yet one of them be right and the other wrong with respect to a case which they can both equally discriminate from other cases. Moral blindness is not (or is not principally) a matter of perceiving two situations as indistinguishable in value which others perceive as having different values; it consists rather in assigning the *wrong* value to a situation which the judger can morally distinguish from other situations as well as the next man.[45]

To this he adds the following further observation:

> ... it is often proper to criticise someone on moral grounds for making *too many* moral distinctions – for making moral distinctions where there are no moral differences: but it would be senseless to criticise someone's colour perception on the ground that his visual system divides the spectrum into more colours than ours does, since the making of (systematic) colour distinctions is *constitutive* of there being corresponding colour differences.[46]

I don't think that anybody would want to disagree with McGinn when he says that 'superiority of moral judgement does not consist solely in the ability merely to make *more* discriminations than others'. And if superiority in *colour* judgment consisted '*solely* in the ability *merely* to make more discriminations' then, surely, the analogy between moral deficiencies and colour blindness would break down. But I can't see why anyone should think that superiority in colour judgment consisted *solely* in this sort of ability.

McGinn might claim that it follows from his, apparently uncontroversial, diagnosis of colour-blindness that superiority in colour judgments just consists in being able to make more discriminations than others. But to claim this is like claiming that, because pneumonia is a matter of having infections in the lungs, good health just consists in not suffering from lung infection. The most that can be inferred from McGinn's diagnosis of colour-blindness is that among persons who *otherwise* have a normal ability to make colour judgments superiority in colour judgments consists in being able to make more discriminations than others.

However, there is clearly more to the ability to make colour judgments than being able to make fine-grained colour discriminations. One must, for example, also be able to group different colours together as shades of red, yellow, blue and so on. The ability to see that two shades of for example red are shades of the 'same' colour seems to be just as essential to the ability to make colour judgments as the ability to distinguish the two shades from each other.

It is possible to imagine a person who, even though he is able to make just as many colour discriminations as anyone else, is in certain sense colour-blind: he lacks the ability to group the different colours that he sees together under more general colour concepts such as red, orange, yellow, brown, green, blue etc. For example, if he is given a number of objects, some of which have colours we would classify as shades of yellow and the rest of which we would see as shades of green, he will not be able to sort them out in yellows and greens. And this is so even if we show him one yellow object and say that those in the first group should be like that one, and similarly show him a green object and tell him that the things in the other group should be of that colour. On the other hand, whenever his ability to distinguish colours is checked he comes out as perfectly normal.[47]

Wouldn't it be reasonable to say of such a person that even though he can see colour differences he can in a certain crucial sense not see the colours that we can see? I think it would, but then it follows that McGinn is wrong in assuming that superiority in colour judgment consists 'solely in the ability merely to make more discriminations than others'. As soon as it is seen that superiority in colour judgment is at least a two-dimensional affair, it becomes easier to imagine ways in which deficiency in moral judgment can be accounted for by analogy with deficiency in colour judgment.

There seem to be two dimensions, comparable to the two dimensions in the ability to make colour judgments just outlined, in which a person can be superior or deficient in his ability to make moral judgments. The first is the ability to distinguish things and actions by reference to different specific moral concerns, concerns corresponding to the specific or, as they are sometimes called, 'thick' moral concepts. These are concepts like 'loyal', 'honest', 'unkind' etc. The second dimension is the ability to see whether something is morally right or wrong, whether it morally ought or ought not to be done; this ability concerns the application of more 'general' or 'thin' moral concepts, i.e. 'good', 'right' etc. Most accounts of the use of general moral concepts take it for granted that whenever a general concept is applied to a thing or an action it must always be possible to back this up by reference to a more specific concern.

So it will be possible to imagine two sorts of 'moral blindness': one that concerns the ability to apply specific moral concepts, a deficiency which consists in applying fewer such concepts and therefore making fewer and coarser moral discriminations than others do; and one that concerns the ability to apply the general moral concepts, a deficiency which consists in being unable to weigh or 'sum up' the specific concerns, or at least in being unable to do so in the right way. It might be thought that the first sort of moral blindness automatically entails the second sort and that the two sorts of deficiences are not independent in the way in which the two types of colour-blindness appear to be independent. But this need not be so. When the general concepts are applied some specific concerns usually carry much more weight than others. And it is easy to imagine someone who makes very crude moral distinctions in terms of the specific moral concepts, but who, because he is aware of which specific concerns generally carry the most weight, nonetheless in most cases arrives at the right decision as to which general concepts apply to the situation.

Given this distinction between two sorts of 'moral blindness, it is, I think, fairly obvious how an adherent of the perceptual paradigm might reply to McGinn's argument. The argument is based on the claim that it is not possible to account for the following sort of moral error by analogy with colour-blindness: 'Two people could in principle be capable of making equally fine-grained moral distinctions, and yet one of them be right and the other wrong with respect to a case which they can both equally discriminate from other cases'. However, this might be accounted for by saying that although neither of the two persons involved suffers from the first of the two kinds of 'moral blindness' distinguished, one of them suffers from the second kind. The morally blind person is unable to weigh or 'sum up' the specific concerns in the right way, and therefore applies the wrong general concept.

McGinn's further observation can, as far as I can see, be dealt with in a similar manner. It is 'proper to criticise someone on moral grounds for making *too many* moral distinctions', if the many distinctions make the person himself or other people whom he might influence blind to the weight of what is, morally speaking, the most *important* feature of the situation that is being assessed. It is a psychological fact that concerns which are not entirely without significance, but whose significance is nonetheless marginal, can, just by being considered, be given too much consideration.[48] Furthermore, someone who is bringing up children, or is otherwise in a position to influence the moral sensibility of other persons, might, by drawing their attention to moral distinctions of only slight significance, influence unfavourably their ability to add up the specific concerns and decide what is morally right and wrong.[49]

In the quotation above McGinn also claims that it often is 'proper to criticise someone ... for making moral distinctions where there are no moral differences', whereas no similar criticism would be appropriate concerning colour-judgments. But the last part of the claim cannot be right. Let us take one of McGinn's Martians. Assume that on the basis of visual experience he systematically distinguishes between things which, as far as we humans can see, have exactly the same colour, say a blue one. Assume, furthermore, that it is found out that what enables him to do this is that his eyes are sensitive not only to light from the visible part of the spectrum but also to ultra-violet rays. Should we then say that the things in questions do not have the same colour, but are really different shades of blue which we, unlike him, are not able to distinguish? Or should we say that what makes him distinguish between the things, viz. differences in reflection of ultra-violet rays, is something that is not relevant to their colour? I think the latter reply is by far the most reasonable; and, if I am right in this, then it would indeed be proper to criticise (in a polite manner, of course) the Martian for making colour distinctions where there are no differences in colour.

So McGinn's argument to the effect that 'moral blindness' cannot be accounted for by analogy with colour blindness does not work. It can be refuted on the basis of the observation that there could be other sorts of colour-blindness than those consisting in being unable to make as many colour discriminations as normal people can make. Whether all moral disagreements of the sort which cause trouble to a dispositional theory are in fact cases of 'moral blindness' is, of course, a different question.[50]

Notes

1. *Cf.* C.G. Hempel, 'The Empiricist Criterion of Meaning', in A.J. Ayer (ed.), *Logical Positivism* (London: Allen & Unwin, 1959), pp. 108-129.
2. *Cf.* J. McDowell, 'Aesthetic Value, Objectivity, and the Fabric of the World', in E. Shaper (ed.), *Pleasure, Preference and Value* (Cambridge: CUP, 1983), pp. 1-16; 'Are Moral Requirements Hypothetical Imperatives?', *The Aristotelian Society*, Supp. Vol. 52, 1978, pp. 13-29; 'Critical Notice', *Mind*, 95, 1986, pp. 377-386; 'Non-Cognitivism and Rule-Following', in S.H. Holtzman & C.M. Leich (eds.), *Wittgenstein: to Follow a Rule* (London, Boston & Henley: RKP, 1981), pp. 141-162; 'The Role of Eudaimonia in Aristotle's Ethics', in A.O. Rorty (ed.), *Essays 0n Aristotle's Ethics* (Berkeley & Los Angeles: University of California Press, 1980), pp. 359-376; 'Values and Secondary Qualities', in T.Honderich (ed.), *Morality and Objectivity* (London, Boston, Melbourne & Henley: RKP, 1985), pp. 110-129; 'Virtue and Reason', *The Monist*, 62, 1979, pp. 331-350. There are parallel and complementary (not necessarily perceptual) ideas in S. Hurley, 'Objectivity and Disagreement', in *Morality and Objectivity*, pp. 54-97; and D. Wiggins, *Needs, Values, Truth* (Oxford: Blackwell, 1987), Essays II-VI & Postscript.
3. J. McDowell, 'Virtue and Reason', pp. 331-332.
4. It should be noted that the analogy between moral thought and perception according to McDowell is not to be taken literally; cf. 'Values and Secondary Qualities', p. 111:

   The perceptual model is no more than a model: perception, strictly so called, does not mirror the role of reason in evaluative thinking, which seems to require us to regard the apprehension of value as an intellectual rather than a merely sensory matter.
5. J. McDowell, 'Aesthetic Value, Objectivity, and the Fabric of the World', p. 5.
6. That our moral thinking gives an erroneous picture of itself has been claimed by J.L. Mackie; *cf.* his *Ethics. Inventing Right and Wrong* (Harmondsworth: Penguin, 1977), p. 35 & pp. 48-49.
7. For a discussion of the implications of the phenomenological claim and further references *cf.* J. Dancy, 'Two Conceptions of Moral Realism', I, *Proceedings of the Aristotelian Society*, Supp. Vol. 60, 1986, pp. 172-173; *cf.* also C. Wright, 'Moral Values, Projection and Secondary Qualities', *Proceedings of the Aristotelian Society*, Supp. Vol. 62, 1988, pp. 11-13.
8. On the Kantian account of moral objectivity *cf.* B. Williams, 'Ethics and the Fabric of the World', in *Morality and Objectivity*, p. 206. For Hare's recent views *cf. Moral Thinking* (Oxford: Clarendon, 1981); and 'Ontology in Ethics', in *Morality and Objectivity*, pp. 39-53, see especially p. 52.
9. J. McDowell, 'Values and Secondary Qualities', p. 110, *cf.* also J.L. Mackie, *Ethics, Inventing Right and Wrong*, pp. 30-35.
10. *Cf.* for example, R.B. Brandt, *Ethical Theory* (Englewood Cliffs, N.J.: Prentice-Hall, 1959), Chs. 7-9; W.K. Frankena, *Ethics* (Englewood Cliffs, N.J.: Prentice-Hall, 1963 & 1973), Ch. 6; and J. Hospers, *Human Conduct* (New York: Hartcourt, Brace & World, 1961), Ch. 11.
11. For a good, critical, discussion of this argument *cf.* S. Blackburn, 'Moral Realism', in J. Casey (ed.), *Morality and Moral Reasoning* (London: Methuen, 1971), pp. 102-105.
12. J. McDowell, 'Non-Cognitivism and Rule-Following', p. 142.
13. *Cf.* J. McDowell, 'Aesthetic Value, Objectivity, and the Fabric of the World'; 'Non-Cognitivism and Rule-Following'; 'Values and Secondary Qualities'; D. Wiggins, 'Truth, Invention and the Meaning of Life', *Proceedings of the British Academy*, 62, 1976, pp. 331-378, reprinted in *Needs, Values, Truth* , pp. 87-137; 'A Sensible Subjectivism?', in *Needs, Values, Truth*, pp. 185-214.

14. The analogy between secondary qualities and values has also been used by some philosophers to show that there are no objective moral facts. They argue that moral values, since they are subjective in the sense specified, are subjective in the following further sense: the phenomenology gives us a wrong picture; the moral properties that things or actions appear to have are only 'projected' onto them on the basis of sensations which do not represent real properties of things and actions; and in so far as we ascribe moral properties to them we are systematically in error. Hume seems to have held such a view, *cf. Treatise of Human Nature*, ed. L.A. Selby-Bigge (Oxford: OUP, 1960), Bk. III, Pt. i, Sec. i, p. 469; more recently John Mackie has defended error theories concerning both values and secondary qualities, *cf.* J.L. Mackie, *Ethics, Inventing Right and Wrong*, Ch. 1; and *Problems from Locke* (Oxford: Clarendon, 1976), pp. 7-36.
15. P. Sandøe, 'Secondary Qualities – Subjective and Intrinsic', *Theoria*, 54, 1988, pp. 200-219.
16. Such a view has been held by among others Hobbes, Hutcheson and Edward Westermarck. For a modern, sympathetic, discussion of the view see D.H. Monro, *Empiricism and Ethics* (Cambridge: CUP, 1967), especially Ch. 4. For a discussion of Westermarck's view see R.B. Brandt, *Ethical Theory*, pp. 166-169. For other examples *cf.* above, Ch. 1, note 18.
17. By saying of a property that it is 'relative' I mean that it at the same time can be true of a thing that it has the property (relative to one person, perspective or perceiver) and that it does not have the property (relative to another person, perspective or perceiver). This use is in accordance with the way in which the term 'relative' is used in most modern literature on ethics.
18. C.D. Broad, 'Some Reflections on Moral-Sense Theories in Ethics', reprinted in D.R. Cheney (ed.), *Broad's Critical Essays in Moral Philosophy* (London: Allen & Unwin, 1971), pp. 188-222.
19. R. Firth, 'Ethical Absolutism and the Ideal Observer', *Philosophy and Phenomenological Research*, 12, 1951-1952, p. 324.
20. *Cf.* R. Firth, 'Ethical Absolutism and the Ideal Observer', pp. 333-335.
21. J. McDowell, 'Values and Secondary Qualities', p. 118.
22. A similar interpretation is given by J.Dancy, 'Two Conceptions of Moral Realism', I, *Proceedings of the Aristotelian Society*, Supp. Vol. 60, 1986, pp. 167-187, see especially pp. 184-185; and by A.H. Goldman, 'Red and Right', *The Journal of Philosophy*, 84, 1987, pp. 349-362, see especially p. 351; cf. also note 4 above.
23. J. McDowell, 'Virtue and Reason', p. 347.
24. R. Firth, 'Ethical Absolutism and the Ideal Observer', p. 330.
25. R.B. Brandt, 'The Definition of an "Ideal Observer" Theory in Ethics', *Philosophy and Phenomenological Research*, 15, 1954-1955, p. 407; *cf.* also Brandt, *Ethical Theory*, pp. 173-176.
26. For an excellent exposition and criticism of Moore's view see C.M. Korsgaard, 'Two Distinctions in Goodness', *The Philosophical Review*, 92, 1983, pp. 169-195.
27. This is not to say that the subjectivist cannot allow any sort of moral disagreement; on the subjectivist view two persons can clearly disagree about the moral judgments of one person.
28. For the classical statement of the view that subjectivists can explain ethical disagreement *cf.* C.L. Stevenson, 'Moore's Arguments against Certain Forms of Naturalism', in P.A. Schilpp (ed.), *The Philosophy of G.E. Moore*, Library of Living Philosophers, Vol. IV (Evanston, Ill.: Northwestern University Press, 1942), pp. 71-90.
29. The claim on which this is based, i.e. that there is a necessary or 'internal' link between morality and motivation, is, of course, highly controversial. It has been disputed by various intuitionists and ethical naturalists, most forcefully in an influential paper by Philippa Foot,

'Morality as a System of Hypothetical Imperatives', *Philosophical Review*, 81, 1972, pp. 305-316; reprinted in P. Foot, *Virtues and Vices* (Oxford: Basil Blackwell, 1978), pp. 157-173; J. McDowell has criticized this paper in 'Are Moral Requirements Hypothetical Imperatives?'; for good discussion of the underlying issue *cf.* W.K. Frankena, 'Obligation and Motivation in Recent Moral Philosophy', in A.I. Melden, *Essays in Moral Philosophy* (Seattle: University of Washington Press, 1958), pp. 40-81.

30. *Cf.* P. Foot, 'Moral Beliefs', reprinted in *Virtues and Vices* (Oxford: Blackwell, 1978), pp. 110-131, and her own later comments to that paper, also in *Virtues and Vices*, pp. xii-xiii.
31. *Cf.* note 12 and D. Wiggins, 'A Sensible Subjectivism?', pp. 198-199.
32. For criticisms of intuitionism based on this point *cf.* R.B. Brandt, *Ethical Theory*, Ch. 8; W.D. Hudson, *Modern Moral Philosophy* (London & Basingstoke: Macmillan, 1970), pp. 100-105.
33. G. Harman, *The Nature of Morality* (New York: OUP, 1977), p. 49; the quoted argument is directed specifically against Firth's ideal observer theory.
34. *Cf.* C. Peacocke, *Sense and Content* (Oxford: Clarendon, 1983), Ch. 2.
35. *Cf.* R. Kirk, 'Goodbye to Transposed Qualia', *Proceedings of the Aristotelian Society*, 82, 1981/82, pp. 33-44.
36. *Cf.* D. Wiggins, 'A Sensible Subjectivism?', §4 & §9; and J. McDowell, 'Aesthetic Value, Objectivity, and the Fabric of the World', pp. 10-11.
37. I am aware that some philosophers of language, notably Quine and Dummett, aspire to give explanations which break out of the circle.
38. *Cf.* W.S. Quinn, 'Moral and other Realisms: Some Initial Difficulties', in A.I. Goldman & J. Kim (eds.), *Values and Morals* (Dordrecht: Reidel, 1978), pp. 257-273.
39. P. Sandøe, 'Secondary Qualities – Subjective and Intrinsic', pp. 209-213.
40. Even across cultures and languages; *cf.* B. Berlin & P. Kay, *Basic Color Terms* (University of California press: Berkeley and Los Angeles, 1969).
41. G. Harman, *The Nature of Morality*, pp. 45-46.
42. J. McDowell, 'Non-Cognitivism and Rule-Following', p. 157.
43. S. Blackburn, 'Errors and the Phenomenology of Value', in T. Honderich (ed.), *Morality and Objectivity*, p. 14.
44. C. McGinn, *The Subjective View* (Oxford: Clarendon, 1983), p. 152-152.
45. C. McGinn, *The Subjective View*, pp. 151-152.
46. C. McGinn, *The Subjective View*, p. 152, n. 39.
47. Some people actually suffer from a sort of colour-blindness very much like the one here imagined. For further details about these so-called anomalous trichomats *cf.* L.M. Hurvich, *Color Vision* (Sunderland, Massachussetts: Sinauer Associates, 1981), Ch. 16.
48. *Cf.* R. Gay, 'Ethical Pluralism: A Reply to Dancy', *Mind*, 94, 1985, p. 253.
49. *Cf.* R.M. Hare, *The Language of Morals*, Ch. 4.
50. I am very grateful to Finn Collin, Troels Engberg-Pedersen, Ingmar Persson, Paul Robinson and David Wiggins for helpful criticism of earlier drafts of this.

Danish Yearbook of Philosophy, Vol. **27** (1992), 72-92

ÜBER DAS VERHÄLTNIS ZWISCHEN IMMANUEL KANTS RECHTS- UND MORALPHILOSOPHIE.

Mogens Chrom Jacobsen
University of Copenhagen

I

Was Kants Rechtsphilosophie betrifft, ist das etwas Kuriose geschehen, dass eine kantianische Rechtsphilosophie schon mehrfach vor Kant geschrieben worden ist. Charakteristisch für diese Versuche, eine kantianische Rechtsphilosophie zu schreiben, etwa die von Fichte und von Heydenreich, ist eine Deduktion des Rechtsgesetzes aus dem kategorischen Imperativ, wie er in der *Grundlegung zur Metaphysik der Sitten* und der *Kritik der praktischen Vernunft* auftritt. Diese Versuche waren in verschiedener Weises sehr problematisch, was jedenfalls von Fichte erkannt wurde. Als Kants eigene Rechtsphilosophie ("Metaphysische Anfangsgründe der Rechtslehre" als erster Teil der *Metaphysik der Sitten*) 1797 erschien, wurde sie mit Entäuschung empfangen, da dieses Werk keinen Deduktionsversuch enthällt.

Ein solcher Deduktionsversuch war aber, so behaupte ich, von Kant nicht intendiert. Eine Verständigung über das Verhältnis zwischen Moral und Recht, wie es in der *Metaphysik der Sitten* auftritt, ist mit dem Begriff der Gesetzgebungsweise verknüpft und man darf die Moralphilosophie der *Metaphysik der Sitten* nicht als eine blosse Fortsetzung der früheren Moralphilosophie, sondern als eine in wesentlichen Aspekten ganz neu ausgearbeitetes Moralphilosophie, ansehen.

Das Recht soll nicht direkt aus dem kategorischen Imperativ abgeleitet werden, obwohl es eine Verbindung zwischen den beiden gibt. Die zwei Gesetzgebungsweisen sind zwei ganz verschiedene Arten, die moralische Dimension in den zwischenmenschlichen Beziehungen zu betrachten, und die eine kann auf die andere nicht zurückgeführt werden, obwohl sie einen gemeinsamen Ausgangspunkt in der praktischen Vernunft haben. Der Schwerpunkt unseres Interesses ist von dem Gesetz selbst auf die Weise der Schaffung des Gesetzes (die Gesetzgebungsweise) zu verlegen.

II

In diesem Abschnitt will ich die voranstehende These ein bisschen näher erörtern und ich will deutlich machen, in welcher Weise ich für meine These argumentieren will.

Dass der wirklich etwas mit der Moralphilosophie geschehen ist zwischen *Grundlegung* (1785) und der *Metaphysik der Sitten* (1797) ergibt sich, aus einem Vergleich zwischen beiden. Zwei Umständen springen in die Augen. Einerseits ist es die Formulierungen des kategorischen Imperativs und andererseits ist es die Distinktion zwischen vollkommenen und unvollkommenen Pflichten.

In der *Grundlegung* behauptet Kant, dass alle drei Formen des kategorischen Imperativs gleich sind, wenngleich diese Erklärung auf verbreitete Skepsis gestossen ist. Zu der *Metaphysik der Sitten* ist jedoch diese Auffassung von dem kategorischen Imperativ ganz verlassen, zugunsten eines einzigen kategorischen Imperatives verbunden mit zwei Sub-Prinzipien von Recht und Tugend.

In der *Grundlegung* wird eine Distinktion zwischen vollkommenen und unvollkommenen Pflichten wesentlich im Bezug auf die zwei ersten Formen des kategorischen Imperatives vorgenommen. Diese Distinktion ist aber eine ganz andere in der *Metaphysik der Sitten*; dort wurde sie in enger Verknüpfung mit den beiden Gesetzgebungsweisen vorgenommen.

Die wesentliche Quelle zum Verständnis des kategorischen Imperativs ist die *Grundlegung zur Metaphysik der Sitten*, aber die Erläuterung des kategorischen Imperatives ist hier nicht eindeutig. Ich finde hier mindestens zwei verschiedene Haupterläuterrungen des kategorischen Imperatives, und ich bezeichne die erste als Kontradiktionstheorie und die zweite als Idealtheorie.

Von äusserster Wichtigkeit sowohl in der *Grundlegung* als in der *Metaphysik der Sitten* ist die Idee, dass unser Wille, wenn wir eine unmoralische Maxime für unsere Handlung annehmen, in einen inneren Widerspruch kommt. Die beiden Theorien, die Kontradiktionstheorie und die Idealtheorie, sind Theorien über den Ursprung dieses Widerspruchs.[1] Hinter der Kontradiktionstheorie versteckt sich, was ich als das übliche verständnis von Kants kategorischem Imperativ betrachte. Die Idealtheorie dagegen drückt einen ganz anderen Gedanken aus, der nicht dieselbe Klarheit besitzt, aber doch andere Vorteile hat. Ich will beide Theorien später erörtern.

In der *Grundlegung* ist die erste und in gewissem Sinne die zweite Form des kategorischen Imperatives, sowie die Distinktion zwischen vollkommenen und unvollkommenen Pflichten überwiegend mit der Kontradiktionstheorie verknüpft, aber in der *Metaphysik der Sitten* sind sowohl die Kontradiktionstheorie, als die mit dieser Theorie verknüpfte Distinktion der vollkommenen und unvollkommenen Pflichten ganz verlassen. In Abschnitt III werde ich zeigen, dass diese Wandlungen nichts Zufälliges sind, sondern dass Kant ein Motiv für diese Veränderungen hatte. Ich werde zeigen, dass die Kontradiktionstheorie keine Rechtsphilosophie begrunden kann und dass Kant auf dieses Problem aufmerksam war.

Will man jedoch die Moralphilosphie der *Metaphysik der Sitten* positiv darstellen, ergeben sich doch Probleme, weil Kant nur wenige Worte auf dieses Thema verwendet. Das gegenseitige Verhältnis zwischen den beiden Begriffen der ethischen und rechtlichen Gesetzgebungsweise und das Verhältnis dieser zu Recht- und Tugendpflichten ist im Text angedeutet, ohne dass der Begriff der Gesetzgebungsweise selbst erörtert ist. Ich glaube, dass man sich die Inspiration in der früheren Moralphilosophie holen muss, und dass die Denkweise in der früheren Moralphilosophie in der *Metaphysik der Sitten* aufgespürt werden kann.

In Abschnitt IV werde ich zeigen, dass es möglich ist, dem Begriff der Gesetzgebungsweise einen Inhalt zu geben, und dass das was ich früher die idealtheoretische Auffassung genannt habe, diesen Inhalt erklären kann. Die idealtheoretische Auffassung finde ich teils, in *Grundlegung* teils in *Zum ewigen Frieden* und *Über der Gemeinspruch*.

Das Argument dafür, dass die Moralphilosophie der *Metaphysik der Sitten* so aufzufassen ist, besteht darin, dass damit das gegenseitige Verhältnis der beiden Begriffe der ethischen und rechtlichen Gesetzgebungsweise und das Verhältnis dieser zu Recht- und Tugendpflichten erklärt werden kann.

Ganz davon abgesehen, dass die idealtheoretische Auffassung die Aussagen über die beide Gesetzgebungsweisen in der *Metaphysik der Sitten* erklären kann, vermag die Idealtheorie auch eine interessante Erklärung über die Verschiedenheit von Recht und Moral zu geben, ohne dass das eine von dem anderen abgeleitet zu werden braucht. In Abschnitt V werde ich diese beiden Erklärungen erörtern.

Die wichtigen Begriffe "Begehrungsvermögen", "Bestimmungsgrund", "Willkür", "Legalitet" und "Moralität" sind in einem Appendix erklärt. Diese Begriffe müssen im Verhältnis zu dem was man Kants Handlungstheorie nennen kann, erörtert werden. Nur in diesem Zusammenhang ist es möglich diesen Begriffe einen bestimmten Sinn zu geben.

III

Die wichtigsten Charakteristika der Kontradiktionstheorie, sind, dass der Widerspruch begrifflich ist, und dass er in Verbindung mit einem Prozess der Universalisierbarkeit auftritt. Im Gegensatz zu einem Prozess der Gesetzgebung in seiner beratenden und konstituierenden Funktion liegt der Schwerpunkt hier auf Prinzipien, und das Ideal ist ein Prinzip der absoluten Entscheidung zwischen Gut und Böse. Diese Auffassung ist mit einem Ideal von der Hierarchie der Prinzipien verbunden, sodass man von dem obersten Prinzip sekundäre Prinzipien ableiten kann.

Kant unterscheidet in der *Grundlegung* zwischen vier Arten von Pflichten, die im nachstehenden Schema illustriert sind.

	Pflichten gegen andere	Pflichten gegen sich selbst
Vollkommene Pflichten	(A) z.B.: Die Plicht sein Wort zu halten	(C) z.B.: Die Pflicht nicht Selbstmord zu begehen
Unvollkommene Pflichten	(B) z.B.: Die Plicht Leuten aus der Not zu hilfen	(D) z.B.: Die Pflicht seine Talente zu entwickeln

Dieses Schema ist angewandt auf die erste und die zweite Form des kategorischen Imperativs, aber nur (A) und (B) der ersten Form des kategorischen Imperativs sind wirklich Ausdruck einer kontradiktionstheoretischen Auffassungsweise.

Onora O'Neill bietet in ihrer Schrift: "Consistency in action", eine ausserordentlich gute Paraphrasierung des Inhalts (A) und (B).

(A) Denn die Allgemeinheit eines Gesetzes, dass jeder, nachdem er in Not zu sein glaubt, versprechen könne was ihm einfällt, mit dem Vorsatz, es nicht zu halten, würde das Versprechen und den Zweck, den man damit haben mag, selbst unmöglich machen, indem niemand glauben würde, dass ihm was versprochen sei, sondern über alle solche Äusserung, als eitles Vorgeben, lachen würde.[2]

(A') A maxim of deceiving others as convenient has as its universalized counterpart the maxim that everyone will deceive others as convenient. But if everyone were to deceive others as convenient then there would be no such thing as trust or reliance on others' acts of communication, hence nobody could be deceived, hence nobody could deceive others as convenient.[3]

(B) Denn ein Wille, der dieses beschlösse, würde sich selbst widerstreiten, indem der Fälle sich doch manche eräugnen können, wo er anderer Liebe und Teilnehmung bedarf, und wo er, durch ein solches aus seinem eigenen Willen entsprungenes Naturgesetz, sich selbst alle Hoffnung des Beistandes, den er sich wünscht, rauben würde.[4]

(B') If I seek to will a maxim of non-beneficence as a universal law, my underlying intention is (not) to help others when they need it and its universalized counterpart is that nobody help no others when they need it. But if everybody denies help to others when they need it, then those who need help will not be helped, and in particular I will not myself be helped when I need it. But if I am committed to the standards of rational willing which comprise the various Principles of Rational Intending, then I am committed to willing some means to any end to which I am committed, and this must include willing that if I am in need of help and therefore not able to achieve my ends without help I be given some appropriate help. In trying to universalize a maxim of non-beneficence I find myself committed simultaneously to willing that I not be helped when I need it and that I be helped when I need it.[5]

(Das Eingeklammerte 'not', findet man im originalen Text nicht, ich vermute aber, dass die Auslassung von 'not' ein Druckfehler ist.)

(A) und (B) entsprechen auch der Distinktion zwischen vollkommenen und unvollkommenen Pflichten. Über vollkommene Pflichten sagt Kant: "Einige Handlungen sind so beschaffen, dass ihre Maxime ohne Widerspruch nicht einmal als allgemeines Naturgesetz gedacht werden kann; weit gefehlt, dass man noch wollen könne, es sollte ein solches werden."[6] Und über unvollkommene Pflichten: "... zwar (ist) jene innere Unmöglichkeit nicht anzutreffen, aber es ist doch unmöglich, zu wollen, dass ihre Maxime zur Allgemeinheit eines Naturgesetzes erhoben werde, weil ein solcher Wille sich selbst widersprechen würde."[7]

Kant sagt auch in dieser Verbindung, dass er im Hinblick auf eine zukünftige *Metaphysik der Sitten* einen Vorbehalt mache, und meint natürlich, dass in der zukünftigen *Metaphysik der Sitten* eine Distinktion zwischen vollkommenen und unvollkommenen Pflichten sehr wichtig ist, da es notwendig ist, Recht und übrige Moral getrennt zu halten. Aber Kants Distinktion in der *Grundlegung* kann diese Aufgabe nicht lösen und deswegen der Vorbehalt.

Auch O'Neill hebt hervor, dass der kategorische Imperativ in dieser Interpretation ein Prinzip ist für diejenigen, die handeln und nicht für diejenigen, die die Handlungen anderer betrachten und beurteilen.[8] Man muss beachten, dass nur grundsätzliche Intentionen universalisiert werden können. Benützt man spezielle Intentionen wie: "Ich will andere Leute betrügen, wenn es mir passt, und wenn ich davonkommen kann", dann funktioniert das Prinzip nicht.

Wenn ich nicht wünsche, ein Ding zu kaufen, das von anderen Leuten gestohlen worden ist, ist es eine grundsätzliche Intention, und daraus können andere Sub-Intentionen abgeleitet werden. Z.B. "Den Verkäufer zu fragen woher kommt diese Ware?", usw. Aber für eine dritte Person, die bei diesem Handel anwesend ist, ist es sehr schwierig zu wissen, ob der Käufer die Intention habe, einen billigeren Preis zu erreichen, oder ob er wirklich nicht wünsche, eine gestohlene Ware zu kaufen.

Mehrere übergeordneten Intentionen können auf diese Weise mit der phänomenalen Beschreibung ein und derselben Handlung vereinbar sein. Sollte man innerhalb eines Rechtssystems beweisen müssen, dass irgendjemand eine bestimmte Intention gehabt habe, würden nur wenige Personen von diesem Gericht verurteilt werden. Jedes Recht muss von einer faktischen Handlung ausgehen, und wenn klar geworden ist, dass der Angeklagte keine böse Intention gehabt hat, muss diese Tatsache ins Urteil mit einbezogen werden. Die Kontradiktionstheorien können aber einen solchen Ausgangpunkt nicht zulassen und können deswegen, eine Rechtsphilosophie nicht begründen.

IV

Mit der Idealtheorie verhält es sich ganz anders. Die Idealtheorie versucht, das Ziel der Moral zu beschreiben, und der Widerspruch ist in dieser Verbindung ein Widerspruch zwischen dem Privatwillen (privates Interesse) und dem allgemeinen Willen (moralisches Ideal). Das Ziel ist die Harmonie zwischen allen Zwecken der Menschen, aber welches Räsonnement führt uns zu diesem Ideal? Kant sagt, dass man sich allgemeine Gesetze vorstellen soll, die von allen Privatzwecken abstrahieren. Was Kant damit meint, will ich später zu erläutern versuchen. Dieses Räsonnement kann sowohl in einer persönlischen Weise als in einer kollektiven Weise durchgefuhrt werden, deswegen die beiden Gesetzgebungsweisen.

Wenn Kant über die beiden Gesetzgebungsweisen spricht, was sagt er dann? Folgende Illustration soll dies etwas klarer machen:

		Gesetz: Der kategorische Imperativ
Ethische Gesetzgebung:	—>	———
———————————		Triebfeder: Pflicht
Recht- und Tugendpflichten		

		Gesetz: Der Rechtsgesetz
Rechtliche Gesetzgebung:	—>	———
———————————		Triebfeder: Zwang
Rechtpflichten		

Zu jeder Gesetzgebung gehören sowohl ein Gesetz als eine Triebfeder und die Triebfeder ist das grundsätzliche Motiv für das Handeln; sie lässt die Gesetzgebungsweise zu oder gebietet sie.[9]

Die ethische Gesetzgebungsweise ist mit dem Motiv der Pflicht in enger Weise verknüpft. Will man ethisch von seinem Willen her gesetzgeben, muss man einem ethischen Räsonnnement folgen, damit man erfahren kann, worin die Pflicht in den gegenwärtigen Umständen besteht und nachfolgend handeln. Handelt man gesetzmässig aus Pflicht, so hat die Handlung nach Kants redeweise Moralität. Der Begriff einer ethischen Gesetzgebungsweise enthällt sowohl eine Beschreibung des Motivs durch Moralität als eine Beschreibung der Handlung als gesetzmässig, was in Kants Redeweise Legalität ist.[10] Alle Pflichten können ethisch Gefolgt werden. Aus dem ethischen Räsonnement ergeben sich alle Pflichten.[11]

Das Gesetz der ethischen Gesetzgebungsweise ist der kategorische Imperativ, und er heisst: "handle nach einer Maxime, welche zugleich als ein allgemeines Gesetz gelten kann" (bzw.: "werden könne"). Die Bestimmung der ethischen Maximen ist hier bloss negativ, da man zuerst seine Maximen nach ihrem subjektiven Ursprung betrachten, und danach untersuchen muss, ob diese Maxime auch als eine allgemeine Gesetzgebung qualifiziert ist.[12]

Die Maximen sind eine Verknüpfung von Zweck und Handlung. Wenn man diesen Zweck will, muss man auch diese Handlung ausführen. Was man hier universalisieren soll, muss den Zweck sein. Dieser Zweck ist die grundsätzliche Intention, die vorher diskutiert worden ist, und weil man weder diese Intention von aussen identifizieren, noch die moralische Gesinnung erzwingen kann, kann die ethische Gesetzgebungsweise nicht als Grundlage einer äusseren Gesetzgebung dienen.[13]

Will man eine äusserlische Gesetzgebung haben, muss man das Räsonnnement der rechtlichen Gesetzgebungsweise anwenden. Die rechtliche Gesetzgebungsweise ist mit Zwang in enger Weise verknüpft. Das Recht fordert eine allgemeine Gesetzgebung, die man mit Zwang durchführen kann. Das Recht fordert nur Legalität, das Motiv der Handlung ist ganz gleichgültig.[14]

Das Gesetz der rechtlichen Gesetzgebung ist das Rechtsgesetz, und das heisst: "Handle äusserlich so, dass der freie Gebrauch deiner Willkür mit der Freiheit von jedermann nach einem allgemeinen Gesetze zusammen bestehen könne."[15] Das Recht beschäftigt sich nur mit äusseren Handlungen, denn nur auf Grund einer allgemeinen Beschreibung der phänomenalen Kennzeichnungen bei Handlungen, die geboten oder nicht erlaubt sind, ist es möglich von einer äusseren Betrachtung her über Recht und Unrecht zu urteilen.

Die Pflichten, die dem rechtlichen Imperativ folgen, sind auch ethische Pflichten, weil man auch diese Pflichten ethisch befolgen kann, was nur eine Frage des Motiv ist. Was bei den Rechtspflichten eigentümlich ist, ist ihre Fähigkeit, erzwungen zu werden, aber nur die Handlung selbst kann erzwungen werden.

Die Pflichten, die der rechtlichen und der ethischen Gesetzgebungsweise gemeinsam sind, sind sowohl dem rechtlichen als auch dem ethischen Räsonnement zugänglich, aber es ist nicht möglich, das eine Räsonnement aus dem anderen abzuleiten.

Die Pflichten die nicht Rechtspflichten sind, sind Tugendpflichten, und Pflichten sind entweder Rechts- oder Tugendpflichten. Die Tugendpflichten können nur einem ethischen Räsonnement folgen und können somit nicht erzwungen werden.[16]

Das Tugendprinzip heisst: "Handle nach einer Maxime der Zwecke, die zu haben für jedermann ein allgemeines Gesetz sein kann." Man muss sich einen Zweck, der zugleich Pflicht ist, vorstellen. Im allgemeinen hat man einen Zweck mit seiner Handlung, und nachher untersucht man, ob dieser Zweck auch moralisch ist, aber bei der Tugend gibt es spezifische Zwecke, die durch die praktische Vernunft festgelegt sind. Zwecke die in sich selbst moralisch sind.[17]

Aus dem, was Kant in der *Metaphysik der Sitten* über die beiden Gesetzgebungsweisen sagt, lässt sich nur wenig über den eigentlichen Inhalt dieser

Gesetzgebungsweise herleiten. Was Kant aber in der *Grundlegung* über ein Reich der Zwecke sagt, und was Kant in dem Abschnitt über das öffentliche Recht in der *Metaphysik der Sitten* über den "vereinigten Willen" sagt, gibt uns eine Idee davon, was er mit diesen Begriffen meint.

Er sagt folgendes über das Reich der Zwecke in der *Grundlegung*:

> Ich verstehe aber unter einem Reiche die systematische Verbindung verschiedener vernünftiger Wesen durch gemeinschaftliche Gesetze. Weil nun Gesetze die Zwecke ihrer allgemeinen Gültigkeit nach bestimmen, so wird, wenn man von dem persönlichen Unterschiede vernünftiger Wesen, imgleichen allem Inhalte ihrer Privatzwecke abstrahiert, ein Ganzes aller Zwecke (sowohl der vernünftigen Wesen als Zwecke an sich, als auch der eigenen Zwecke, die ein jedes sich selbst setzen mag), in systematischer Verknüpfung, d.i. ein Reich der Zwecke gedacht werden können, welches nach obigen Prinzipien möglich ist.[18]

Hier ist ganz besonders zu bemerken: Einerseits die gesetzliche Natur der moralischen Gemeinschaft, und andererseits das Abstrahieren von den Privatzwecken. Was meint er eigenlich mit dem Abstrahieren von den Privatzwecken? Folgendes Zitat trägt zu klärung bei:

> Denn der, den ich durch ein solsches Versprechen zu meinen Absichten brauchen will, kann unmöglich in meine Art, gegen ihn zu verfahren, einstimmen und also selbst den Zweck dieser Handlung enthalten.[19]

Wenn man einstimmen kann, gegen einen anderen in einer bestimmten Weise zu Verfahren, muss diese Einstimmung eine rationelle Einstimmung sein. Das Gesetz eines Verfahrens muss ein Gesetz sein, dem alle zustimmen können. Wann können aber alle einem Gesetz zustimmen d.i. einem Gesetz in einer rationellen Weise zustimmen? Eine rationelle Einstimmung ist eine Einstimmung unter der Bedingung des Abstrahierens von den Privatzwecken. Wenn ich in einer bestimmten Situation stehe, wo ich ein Versprechen abgegeben habe, muss ich überlegen, ohne meine Privatzwecke hineinzumischen, ob ich in einer rationellen Weise, dieses Verfahren allgemein machen kann. Wird es rationeller sein, dieses Verfahren zu wählen als ein alternatives?

Die Frage ist darum die folgende: Welches rationelle Vorgehen führt zu der Maxime, die allgemein gemacht werden kann? Kant hat diese Frage nicht beantwortet, der amerikanische Philosoph John Rawls hat aber in seinem Buch *A Theory of Justice* versucht, diese Frage auf einer kantianischen

Grundlage zu beantworten.[20] Er hat zur Veranschaulichung dieser Denkungsweise ein Bild gewählt, welches er "den Schleier der Unwissenheit" genannt hat. Die moralischen Prinzipien sind einer rationellen Wahl unterworfen, und die Moralphilosophie ist das Studium der Bedingungen für rationelle Entscheidungen. In der ursprünglischen Position sind alle von einem Schleier der Unwissenheit umgegeben. Das bedeutet, dass niemand weiss, welche natürlische Fähigkeiten oder welche soziale Position er in dieser Welt hat. Wie würden diese Personen unter diesen Umständen und einem zweckmässigen Prinzip der Rationalität aus entscheiden? Bei Rawls ergibt sich hier eine Methode, durch welche man von Privatzwecken abstrahieren, und doch gleichzeitig zu einer Entscheidung darüber kommen kann, welche Maximen allgemein gemacht werden können. Ich will diese Frage nicht weiter erörtern, sondern nur bemerken, dass die Idee einer abstraktion von Privazwecken sich weiter entwickeln kann, und dass diese Idee einen bestimmten Inhalt hat.

Kants Auslegung dieser Idee geschieht in der *Grundlegung* von einem persönlischen Ausgangspunkt her. Der Agierende muss überlegen, ob seine Maxime, auch wenn man von Privatzwecken abstrahiert, rationell sei. Er muss das Räsonnement durchführen, und wenn er es durchführt, hat er auch in eine moralische Denksweise eingewilligt. Dies ist die ethische Gesetzgebungsweise, und man versteht sofort, warum diese Gesetzgebungsweise mit dem moralischen Motiv verknüpft ist.

Die Denksweise Rawls in *A Theory of Justice* ist eine andere, weil er Gesetze für eine ganze Gemeinschaft machen will, und wir finden hier keinen bestimmten Agenten, sondern nur die Gesetze, die die Gemeinschaft als eine kollektive Gesamtheit wählen würde, wenn man von allen Privatzwecken abstrahieren würde. Die Wahl ist hier nicht persönlich sondern kollektiv. Weil es in diesem Räsonnement keinen bestimmten Agenten gibt, hat das Motiv keine Bedeutung.

Diese Denkweise findet man auch bei Kant in dem Abschnitt über das öffentliche Recht in der *Metaphysik der Sitten*. Hier sagt Kant: "Die gesetzgebende Gewalt kann nur dem vereinigten Willen des Volkes zukommen. Denn, da von ihr alles Recht ausgehen soll, so muss sie durch ihr Gesetz schlechterdings niemand unrecht tun können."[21] Der vereinigte Wille des Volkes ist eine a priori Idee, und er ist als gesetzgebende Gewalt, insofern sie dem vereinigten Willen des Volkes gehört, ein Gedankending.[22]

In *Über den Gemeinspruch* ist folgendes zu lesen:

> nämlich jeden Gesetzgeber zu verbinden, dass er seine Gesetze so gebe, als sie aus dem vereinigten Willen eines ganzen Volks haben entspringen können, und jeden Untertan, so fern er Bürger sein will, so anzusehen, als ob er zu einem solchen Willen mit zusammen gestimmet habe. Denn das ist der Probierstein der Rechtmässigkeit eines jeden öffentlichen Gesetzes.[23]

In dem selben Werk kann man auch lesen: "... was ein Volk nicht über sich selbst beschliessen kann, das kann der Gesetzgeber auch nicht über das Volk beschliessen."[24] Im *Zum ewigen Frieden* sagt Kant, dass unsere äussere rechtliche Freiheit erklärt werden kann als eine Befugnis, nicht anderen äusseren Gesetzen zu gehorchen als solchen, denen man auch selbst seine Zustimmung geben kann.[25]

Die Zustimmung von der Kant hier redet, muss eine Zustimmung des Menschen als rationelles Wesen sein und der vereinigte Wille des Volkes kann nur der Wille sein, der übrig ist, wenn man von all dem Zufälligen der einzelnen Personen, d.i. den Privatzwecken abstrahiert hat. Die Rede ist hier von der rechtlichen Gesetzgebungsweise, welche der Hintergrund der ganzen Rechtsphilosophie ist, und der daraus sich ergebende Idealzustand des Rechts ist ausgedrückt in dem, was ich die übergeordnete rechtsphilosophische Idee nenne.

Die übergeordnete rechtsphilosophische Idee ist die Idee der Zusammenstimmung von der Freiheit der Einzelnen mit der Freiheit der anderen nach Gesetzen der Freiheit. Freiheit bedeutet hier, äussere Handlungen ohne Hindernisse auszuführen. Es ist ganz klar, dass man wenn alle wünschen, Handlungen ohne Hindernisse auszuführen, anarchische Zustände haben wird. Die Handlungen müssen einigen Regeln unterworfen werden, aber diese Regeln müssen moralische Regeln sein. Was Kant eigenlich hier sagt, ist, dass die Handlungen der Menschen in der Gesellschaft durch Regeln begrenzt werden müssen, und dass diese Regeln moralisch sein müssen. Was moralisch ist, das zu erklären ist die Aufgabe der rechtlichen Gesetzgebungsweise.

Wenn Kant seine übergeordnete rechtsphilosophische Idee formuliert, benutzt er an verschiedenen Stellen verschiedene Ausdrücke für Freiheit. Hier ist eine kleine Auswahl: "Willkür", "der freie Gebrauch deiner Willkür, "Freiheit", "äussere Freiheit", "Freiheit (Unabhängigkeit von eines anderen nötigender Willkür). Viel Verwirrung bezüglich dieser Frage hat ihren Ursprung in der Tatsache, dass Kant vier verschiedene Begriffe der "Freiheit" anwendet.

In einer Willkür ist das Begehrungsvermögen nach Prinzipien bestimmt. Ist diese Willkür eine solche, dass das Begehrungsvermögen sowohl durch Lust/Unlust als durch Vernunftsprinzipien bestimmt werden kann, redet Kant von "einer freien Willkür" und die Freiheit ist in dieser Beziehung: Freiheit im Sinne von Indeterminismus.

Ist die (freie) Willkür in einer bestimmten Situation eine solche, dass das Begehrungsvermögen durch Vernunftprinzipien bestimmt ist, redet Kant von "der Freiheit der Willkür", und in diesem Sinne benutzt Kant in der *Grundlegung* und im *Kritik der Praktischen Vernunft* den Begriff der "Freiheit". Diese ist die Freiheit des Geistes von den Neigungen.

Es gibt indessen auch eine dritte und vierte Bedeutung von Freiheit, die Kant äussere Freiheit nennt im Gegensatz zu der zweiten, die Kant innere Freiheit nennt. Der Unterschied zwischen diesen zwei verschiedenen Formen der äusseren Freiheit ist in *Zum ewigen Frieden* am besten erklärt. Diese werden hier die gesetzlose Freiheit und die rechtliche Freiheit genannt.

Die äussere rechtliche Freiheit ist in *Zum ewigen Frieden* die "Befugnis, keinen äusseren Gesetze zu gehorschen, als zu denen ich meine Beistimmung habe geben können"[26] Diese Freiheit ist verschieden von der gesetzlosen Freiheit, die die Freiheit ist, die die Menschen hatten, ehe sie sich zu öffentlichen Zwangsgesetzen bequemten.[27]

Ist diese gesetzlose Freiheit aber dieselbe, wie die "Unabhägigkeit von eines anderen nötingender Willkür"? Ich möchte nicht gern einen fünften Begriff der Freiheit einführen. Wenn Kant von gesetzloser Freiheit redet, meint er Freiheit von moralischen Gesetzen in öffentlicher Form, welche eben nicht dieselbe wie "Unabhägigkeit von eines anderen nötingender Willkür" ist. Auch die Menschen im Naturzustand sind von nötingender Willkür der anderen anhängig, z.B. wenn sie im Gefecht sind. Was Kant vermutlich mit gesetzloser Freiheit meint, ist die Freiheit, sich Zwecke zu setzen, sich Handlungen zur Erreichung dieser Zwecke vorzustellen und zu versuchen, diese Handlungen durchzuführen. Diese Auslegung wird zudem von dem Ausdrück "der freie Gebrauch deiner Willkür" unterstützt.

Der Begriff der Freiheit, der in der übergeordneten rechtsphilosophischen Idee auftritt, ist die gesetzlose Freiheit, und die rechtliche Freiheit ist die gesetzlose Freiheit, wenn diese von allgemeinen moralischen Gesetzen (gesellschaftlichen (G)) begrenzt ist. Wenn Kant hier den Ausdrück "Willkür" braucht, wünscht er hervorzuheben, dass das Recht bewusste Handlungen und indeterminierte Wesen, d.i. die Menschen angeht.

Aus der übergeordneten rechtsphilosphischen Idee können vier Rechtsprincipien abgeleitet werden. Das Prinzip der Rechtspflichten, das Prinzip des subjektiven Rechts, das Prinzip der Rechtsprivilegien und das Prinzip des objektiven Rechts.

Im Prinzip der Rechtpflichten wird festgestellt, dass man äusserlich so handeln muss, dass die Übereinstimmung nicht gestört wird. Mit Kants eigenen Worten:

> Handle äusserlich so, dass der freie Gebrauch deiner Willkür mit der Freiheit von jedermann nach einem allgemeinen Gesetze zusammen bestehen könne, ...[28]

Im Prinzip des subjektiven Rechts wird festgestellt, dass man ein subjektives Recht habe, alles zu tun, was die Übereinstimmung nicht störe. Mit Kants eigenen Worten:

> Freiheit (Unabhängigkeit von eines anderen nötigender Willkür),sofern sie mit jedes anderen Freiheit nach einem allgemeinen Gesetz zusammen bestehen kann, ist dieses einzige, ursprüngliche, jedem Menschen, kraft seiner Menschheit, zustehende Recht.[29]

Im Prinzip der Privilegien wird festgestellt, dass alle Handlungen, die die Zusammenstimmung nicht stören, rechte Handlungen sind und nach Hohfelds Redeweise priviligiert sind, worauf ich später zurückkommen werde. Kant sagt über diese Frage folgendes:

> Eine jede Handlung ist recht, die oder nach deren Maxime die Freiheit der Willkür eines jeden mit jedermanns Freiheit nach allgemeinen Gesetze zusammen bestehen kann etc.[30]

Wenn man den Begriff "rechte Handlung" mit den Begriffen der "Recht"/ "Unrecht" und "erlaubt" vergleicht, dann sieht man, dass sie verschieden sind. Über die letzteren Begriffe sagt Kant:

> Aller Pflicht korrespondiert ein Recht, als (falcutas moralis generatim) Befugnis betrachtet, aber nicht aller Pflicht korrespondieren Rechte eines anderen ....., jemand zu zwingen; sondern diese heissen besonders Rechtspflichten.[31]
> Erlaubt ist eine Handlung (licitum), die der Verbindtlichkeit nicht entgegen ist; und diese Freiheit, die durch keinen entgegensetzten Imperativ eingeschränkt wird, heisst die Befugnis (falcutas moralis).[32]

> Recht oder Unrecht ..... überhaupt ist eine Tat, sofern sie pflichtmässig oder pflichtwidrig (factum licitum aut illicitum) ist; die Pflicht selbst mag, ihrem Inhalte oder ihrem Ursprunge nach, sein, von welcher Art sie wolle.[33]

> Es ist unrecht, d.i. es widerstreitet der Pflicht.[34]

Wir haben also zwei Begriffe des Rechts, einerseits Recht als Befugnis zu zwingen, und anderseits Recht als "erlaubt" d.i. der Pflicht nicht widerstreitend. Der Begriff eine "rechte Handlung" ist eine Instanz des Zweiten Begriffes des Rechts, weil Recht (und Unrecht) in dieser Form im Verhältnis zu Pflichten im Allgemeinen definiert ist, während der Begriff der "rechten Handlung" allein im Verhältnis zu Rechtspflichten definiert ist. Ich weiss nicht, ob diese Differenz von seiten Kants vorsätzlich ist, aber der Begriff einer "rechten Handlung" ist mit dem Begriff des "Privilegs" in guter Übereinstimmung, und warum nicht auch ein Begriff eines moralischen Privilegs zum Unterschied von einem blossen rechtlichen Privileg?

Diese drei Prinzipien sind im Prinzip des objektiven Rechts vereint, als der Inbegriff der Bedingungen dieser Übereinstimmung, oder als der Inbegriff von der Gesamtheit aller Regeln, die die menschlichen Verbindungen in der Gesellschaft bestimmen.[35]

Im Rechtsbegriff stecken die Schlüsselbegriffe: Pflichten, Rechte und Privilegien, die analysiert werden können im Sinne von Hohfeld. In seinem Artikel "Fundamental legal conceptions" erklärt Hohfeld die Verbindung zwischen diesen drei Begriffen, und diese Erklärung kann auch auf Kant angewendet werden.[36]

Die Rechte sind immer korrelat zu Pflichten. Gibt es eine Person mit einem Recht, dann gibt es einige oder mehrere Personen, die eine Pflicht haben, dieses Recht zu respektieren. Mit Privilegien verhält es sich anders, ein Privilegium steht im Gegensatz zu Pflicht.

Der Inhaber eines Privilegs hat nicht die Pflicht, das zu unterlassen, worin das Privileg besteht. Das Privileg ist einem 'Nicht-Recht' korreliert. Wenn eine Person ein Privileg hat, ist nichts darüber gesagt, welche Rechte andere haben, nur, dass der Privileg-Inhaber keine Pflicht hat, das zu unterlassen, worin sein Privileg besteht, und wenn es eine solche Pflicht nicht gibt, gibt es natürlich auch kein korrelierendes Recht. Mit einem Privileg ist nicht verbunden, dass andere eine Pflicht haben, das Privileg zu respektieren, gibt es aber eine solche Pflicht, hat sie einen von dem Privileg unabhängigen Ursprung.

Es gibt keine logische Verbindung zwischen dem Besitz eines Privilegium und der Pflicht anderer, dies zu respektieren. Eine Moral die nur verlangt, dass die Leute jeden Sonntag in die Kirche gehen, und eine Mark in den Opferstock zu legen, kann nicht verhindern, dass die Leute sich auf der Strasse verprügeln, obwohl alle Leute das Privileg haben auf der Strasse in Ruhe und Frieden zu spazieren (insofern sie nicht in der Kirche sein sollten).

Die rechtsphilosophische Idee hat enthält aber eine Gegenseitigkeit, sodass alle Privilegien gleichzeitig auch Rechte sind, und von dieser Einsicht her kann man sagen, dass das Prinzip der Rechte auch ein Prinzip der Privilegien ist, was ich aber das Prinzip der Privilegien genannt habe, ist nicht zu verstehen, ohne die Einführung des Begriffs von einem Privileg.

Mit diesen Begriffen der Pflicht, des Rechts und des Privilegs hat man die grundsätzliche Struktur der kantischen Rechtsphilosophie.

V

Das Verhältnis zwischen Kants Rechts- und Moralphilosophie ist das Verhältnis zwischen den beiden Gesetzgebungsweisen. Was sagt aber Kant über dieses Verhältnis und wie sollen wir uns dazu verhalten?

Er sagt, dass alle Rechtspflichten ethisch befolgt werden können und sich aus der ethischen Gesetzgebungsweise ergeben. Alle Pflichten die sich aus der rechtlichen Gestzgebungsweise ergeben, ergeben sich auch aus der ethischen Gesetzgebungsweise, aber nicht umgekehrt. Ein Gesetz (G), das man in einer unparteiishen Weise annehmen kann, muss auch als eine persönliche Handlungsregel gelten können. Doch kann die persönlische Handlungsregel sich sehr spezifischen Situationen anpassen, weil die handelnde Person diese Situation kennt. Ein Gesetz dagegen kann in Praxis nur generelle Situationen in Betracht ziehen, und deswegen gibt es eine Diskrepanz. Dieses Problem ist auch heute bekannt, z.B. obwohl man von einem persönlischen Gesichtspunkt aus in einer bestimmten Situation, aktive Sterbehilfe billigen kann, ist es ganz unmöglich, seiner Zustimmung eine gesetzliche (G) Form zu geben.

Ebenso ist eine persönliche Handlungsregel, die man in einer unparteiischen Weise annehmen kann, nicht notwendigerweise auch Gesetzesfähig (G). Kant sagt, dass die Gesetzgebungsweise für Tugendpflichten ethisch sein muss, dass aber nicht alle Pflichten, die sich aus der ethischen Gesetzgebungsweise ergeben, Tugendpflichten sind. Warum sind Tugendpflichten nicht umsetzbar in äussere Gesetzgebung, und warum muss man Tugendpflichten ethisch befolgen?

Beim Handeln kann man zwischen drei verschiedene Elementen unterscheiden: Die Handlung selbst (die phänomenale Beschreibung), die grundsätzliche Intention (den Zweck) und den Beweggrund der Handlung (den Bestimmungsgrund). Es ist der Beweggrund, der die Frage von der Moralität der Handlung bestimmt, während das Tugendprinzip seinen moralischen Charakter von der grundsätzlichen Intention her erhält. Diese Intention der Menschenliebe und der Selbstentwicklung kann nicht erzwungen werden, denn sobald die Androhung von Zwang wirksam wird, wird der Wunsch, diesem Zwang zu entgehen, die grundsätzliche Intention. Der moralische Zweck muss immer von dem moralischen Beweggrund begleitet werden, denn wenn der Beweggrund nicht ein moralischer sondern ein Beweggrund des Selbstinteresses wäre, dann würde die grundsätzliche Intention nicht eine der Menschenliebe sein, sondern eine Intention des Selbstinteresses, und die Menschenliebe würde nur eine Sub-Intention sein.[37]

Kant sagt, dass alle Pflichten entweder Rechtspflichten oder Tugendpflichten sind, und irgendwie muss der kategorische Imperativ alle Pflichten gebieten, aber gleichzeitig kann man diese Pflichten in zwei verschiedene Arten einteilen.

Im kategorischen Imperativ ist von der Maxime (Zweck und Handlung) eine Allgemeinheit verlangt, die hier als unparteiische Anschauung ausgelegt ist, das Wichtigste hier ist aber der Zweck der Maxime oder die grundsätzliche Intention. Die Menschen setzen sich Zwecke, und die Moral fordert, dass diese allgemein gemacht werden können, unter diesen Zwecken, die allgemein gemacht werden können, gibt es Zwecke, die in sich allgemein sind, und das sind eben die Tugendzwecke. Ich glaube, dass Kants Idee in dieser Verbindung ist, dass die Zwecke der Menschenliebe und der Selbstentwicklung Zwecke sind, die unter allen Umständen in unparteiischer Weise angenommen werden können. Das Recht dagegen redet nur von Handlungen, aber für jede Handlung muss es einen Zweck geben, und deswegen gibt es gleichzeitig einen ethischen und ein rechtlichen Zugang zu denselben Pflichten.

Kant sagt, dass ein Widerstreit der Pflichten nicht möglich ist, ausserdem sagt er, dass die unvollkommenen / Tugendpflichten einen verschiedenen Grad von Unvollkommenheit haben.[39] Er sagt, dass verschiedene Gründe der Verbindlichkeit einander widerstreiten können, obwohl nur der stärkere

Verpflichtungsgrund den Namen von Pflicht erhalten kann, er sagt aber nicht, um welche Gründe es sich handelt. Könnten es die Gründe der Rechtsverpflichtung oder der Tugendverpflichtung sein? Widerstreitet nicht immer der Grund der Tugendverpflichtung der Menschenliebe den Gründe der Rechtsverpflichtungen z.B. im Strafrecht? Kant sagt über die Tugendpflichten, dass die vollkommsten unter den TungendpflichtenVorrecht haben, z.B. die Elternliebe kommt vor der allgemeinen Nächstenliebe. Ausserdem sagt er nur, dass Tugendpflichten verdienstliche Pflichten sind, und dass Rechtspflichten von enger Verbindlichkeit sind, und deswegen meint er vermutlich, dass Rechtspflichten immer Tugendpflichten besiegen. Dafür gibt es aber kein Argument.

Als Illustration des Verhältnisses der beiden Gesetzgebungsweisen, kann folgendes Beispiel dienen.

Ein Mitglied der Volksversammlung in einem demokratischen Staat, das ich in Ermangelung von etwas Besserem P nennen will, steht in einer persönlichen Relation zu seiner Umgebung und nimmt gleichzeitig an der Arbeit teil, eine öffentlische Gesetzgebung zu etablieren und aufrechtzuerhalten.

P überlegt, von einem Freund Geld zu leihen, er ist aber nicht ganz sicher, ob er das Geld zurückbezahlen kanne. Viele Umstände haben in dieser Situation Bedeutung: Weiss der Freund, dass er möglicherweise nicht bezahlen kann, ist er sehr sparsam und genau in Geldangelegenheiten, wie viel Geld wünscht P zu leihen usw. Als eine moralische Person versucht P seine Maxime dem ethischen Räsonnement zu unterwerfen. Wird seine Maxime, auch wenn man sie auf eine unparteiische Weise anschaut eine rationelle sein? P lässt sich auf ein ethisches Räsonnement ein und konkludiert, dass er das Geld nicht leihen will. Dass P sich auf das ethische Räsonnement einlässt, ist Ausdruck des moralischen Bestimmungsgrundes zur Handlung, wenn dieses Räsonnement entscheidend für die Handlung ist. Das Räsonnement und der Bestimmungsgrund sind hier in enger Verbindung. Was das ethische Räsonnement charakterisiert, ist, dass es ausgeht von der konkreten Handlungsmaxime und Handlungssituation einer bestimmten Person, und das Ergebnis dieses Räsonnement ist ein konkreter Handlungsimperativ. Umstände, Räsonnement und Handlung sind im Bewusstsein des Handelnden chronologisch verbunden.

Als Mitglied der Volksversammlung wünscht P so zu handeln, dass nur solche Gesetze entschieden werden, die das Volk über sich selbst entscheiden könnte. Wenn P so denkt, dann ist das ein ethisches Räsonnement, aber wenn P mit dem vorschlag zur Gesetzgebung konfrontiert wird, dann muss er entscheiden, ob das Volk sich selbst aus dies entscheiden könnte, und das ist das rechtliche Räsonnement. Das Räsonnement geht hier nicht von einer bestimmten Handlungssituation aus, sondern von einer generellen Beschreibung, und die Person, die das Räsonnement durchführt, soll nicht nachfolgend in einer bestimmten Weise handeln, weil sich aus diesem Räsonnement kein spezifischer Handlungsimperativ ergibt. Mit diesem Räsonnement ist nur eine allgemeine Beschreibung von verbotenen oder gebietenden Handlungen verbunden, und so kann man kein Motiv mit dem Räsonnement verbinden.

VI

Ich meine, dass es Kant gelungen ist, einen interessanten Zusammenhang zwischen Moral und Recht in der *Metaphysik der Sitten* aufzustellen, aber die Frage, auf welche Weise man Privatzwecken abstrahieren soll, steht immer noch offen. John Rawls hat versucht, diese Frage zu beantworten, Kant aber nicht. In dieser Beziehung kann man sagen, dass die Kontradiktionsauffassung der Idealauffassung überlegen ist, andererseits kann diese nicht das Verhältnis zwischen Moral und Recht erklären.

Die Frage über die Unparteiischkeit liesse sich allerdings in einer ganz anderen Weise angehen. Vielleicht würde Kant uns vorschlagen, die "Harmonie aller Zwecke" als das Ziel der Moral anzusehen und das Mittel dazu würde ein unparteiisches Urteil über Streitfragen sein. In derselben Weise wie das Ziel der Naturwissenschaft eine zusammenhängende Erklärung der Naturphänomene ist, und das Mittel dazu ein vorurteilsfreies Urteil über unsere Erfahrungen ist.

Aber was will es sagen, vorurteilsfrei zu sein? Hinsichtlich dieser Frage haben die Wissenschaftler eine Reihe von pragmatischen aber begründeten Prinzipien aufgestellt, um zu klären, was gute Wissenschaft ist. Warum kann man nicht etwas Ähnliches in der Moral tun? Ich glaube, dass dies möglich ist. Die Interessen der Menschen werden aber in viel höherem Grad Einfluss auf die Urteilskraft haben, wenn es sich um moralische Fragen, als bei naturwissenschaftlichen. Doch hat man auch hier gesehen, dass Interessen die Urteilskraft beeinflusst haben. Man könnte Weiter in dieser Frage forschen und die Prinzipien klären, die wir benützen, um unparteiisch zu urteilen.

APPENDIX

Im gewissen Sinne kann man sagen, dass Kant eine Handlungstheorie hat, und der Ausgangspunkt dieser Theorie ist der Begriff des Begehrungsvermögens und dessen Verbindung mit Gefühl und Vernunft. Das Begehrungsvermögen ist das Vermögen, sich über wünschenswerte Situationen Vorstellungen zu machen. In Verbindung mit dem Begehrungsvermögen steht das Vermögen, bei diesen Vorstellungen Lust oder Unlust zu fühlen. "Gefühle" sind komplexe Äusserungen des Bewusstseins, in welche sowohl ein Element der Erkenntnis (Vorstellung) als ein Element des Gefühls (Lust/Unlust) eingehen. Unsere Gefühle betreffen nur Vorstellungen, und diese Vorstellung wird mit Lust oder Unlust verbunden. Nur unter solchen Umständen wo das Gefühl von Lust oder Unlust eine Vorstellung von äusseren Dingen betrifft, kann man im eigentlichen Sinne von Begehren und Abscheu sprechen, und die Lust oder Unlust sind hier praktisch. Gibt es ein solch äusseres Ding nicht, kann man nur von einer ästhetischen Lust oder Unlust reden, was hier nicht von Interesse ist. Die Bestimmung des Begehrungsvermögens kann mit den beiden Begriffen des Bestimmungsgrundes und des Bestimmungsmodus erklärt werden.

Bestimmungsgrund	LUST (praktisch). Lust als Ursache, Begierde im engen Verstand	REINE VERNUNFT-PRINZIPIEN Lust als Wirkung, moralische Lust (praktisch)
Bestimmungsmodus		
INFOLGE ANLAGE	NEIGUNG	SINNENFREIE NEIGUNG
INFOLGE PRINZIPIEN	INTERESSE DER NEIGUNG	VERNUNFTSINTERESSE

Die praktische Lust/Unlust kann in Verbindung mit Begehren /Abscheu entweder Ursache oder Wirkung sein, und insofern die Lust/Unlust Ursache ist, ist sie Bestimmungsgrund des Begehrungsvermögens, ist sie aber Wirkung, ist das Begehrungsvermögen durch Vernunftsprinzipien bestimmt. Findet man das Begehrungsvermögen durch Anlage bestimmt und nicht von ein Überlegung her, die der Bestimmung des Begehrungsvermögens vorhergeht, dann redet man entweder von Neigung oder von sinnenfreier Neigung. Findet man dagegen das Begehrungsvermögen durch Prinzipien bestimmt, dann redet man entweder von Interesse der Neigung oder von Vernunftsinteresse.[39]

Eine Handlung die sich aus einem Begehrungsvermögen ergibt, das durch Vernunftsprinzipien bestimmt ist, ist die formelle Definition einer Handlung, die von Moralität begleitet ist. Im Handeln kann man zwischen drei verschiedenen Elementen unterscheiden: die Handlung selbst (die phänomenale Beschreibung), die grundsätzliche Intention (der Zweck) und der Beweggrund der Handlung (der Bestimmungsgrund). Die Legalität einer Handlung ist die blosse Übereinstimmung mit dem Moralgesetz, und die blosse Übereinstimmung ist die Übereinstimmung in der äusseren Handlung; sowohl der Zweck als der Bestimmungsgrund sind ohne Bedeutung Trotz des Namens hat die Legalität keine spezielle Verbindung mit dem Recht.

Die Wesen, die nach Prinzipien handeln und zwar bewusst und mit dem Vermögen, das Ziel für ihre Handlungsprinzipien hervorbringen zu können, haben nach Kant Willkür.[40]

Anmerkungen

O = oben, O+ = zwischen oben und mitte, M = mitte, M+ = zwischen mitte und unten, U = unten. Alle Hinweise auf Kants Werke beziehen sich auf Suhrkamp Taschenbuch Wissenschaft, hrsg. von Wilhelm Weischededel, Frankfurt am Main 1974.

MdS = *Metaphysik der Sitten*, GzMdS = *Grundlegung zur Metaphysik der Sitten*, UdG = *Über den Gemeinspruch*, ZeF = *Zum ewigen Frieden*.

1. GzMdS. S. 52-55, 62, spez. S. 54 M, 55 O & M, 70 U.
2. GzMdS. S. 53 M.
3. Onora O'Neill, "Consistency in Action", *Morality and Universality*, eds. N. Potter & M. Timmons, Reidel 1985, S. 174-175.
4. GzMdS. 54 M+.
5. O'Neill S. 177 M.
6. GzMdS. S. 54-55.
7. GzMdS. S. 55 O.
8. O'Neill S. 162-163, 166, 175 M+.
9. MdS. S. 323 M.
10. MdS. S. 324 O+, 324-325, 521 M, 523 U.
11. MdS. S. 325 O+, 326 M.
12. MdS. S. 331 M+, 332 M+, 519 O.
13. MdS. S. 324-325
14. MdS. S. 318 M+, 338-339, 312 U.
15. MdS. S. 338 O+.
16. MdS. S. 347 O, 510 M.
17. MdS. S. 526 M, 510 M, 512 M+, 519 M+, 511-512.
18. GzMdS. S. 66 M.

19. GzMdS. S. 62 O+.
20. John Rawls, *A Theory of Justice*, Harward University Press 1971, paragraph 40.
21. MdS. S. 432 O+.
22. MdS. S. 461 O+.
23. UdG. S. 153 M+.
24. UdG. S. 162 M.
25. ZeF. S. 204 U.
26. ZeF. S. 204 M.
27. ZeF. S 209 M, 212 U, 221 O.
28. MdS. S. 338 M.
29. MdS. S. 345 M+.
30. MdS. S. 337 M+.
31. MdS. S. 512 M.
32. MdS. S. 328 M+.
33. MdS. S. 330 O+.
34. UdG. S. 141 O.
35. MdS. S. 337 M+.
36. W.N. Hohfeld, *Fundamental Legal Conceptions as Applied in Judicial Reasoning*, Yale University Press 1923, S. 36 M, 38-39, 43 O. MdS. S. 512 M.
37. MdS. S. 510-511
38. MdS. S. 330 M+, 520.
39. MdS. S. 315-317.
40. MdS. S. 317-318.

Danish Yearbook of Philosophy, Vol. **27** (1992), 93-108

THE SIGNIFICANCE OF SOME EXPERIMENTAL TESTS OF QUANTUM MECHANICS

JENS BANG
Niels Bohr Institute

I. *Quantum Mechanics*

Some years ago an article in *Physical Review Letters* by Alain Aspect and co-workers in Paris generated a sensationalistic interest in the media, even before publication. It was more or less said that now, finally, the old quarrel between Bohr and Einstein was decided, in favour of Bohr's standpoint.

Before we look at the quarrel in question let us remember, that Bohr and Einstein had *many* discussions about quantum mechanics, in which Einstein in the end had to give in. The subject of most of these discussions may be summarized under the heading of the consistency of quantum mechanics.

A large part of this consistency is ensured by the mathematics. It was certainly important for Bohr that around 1925 it turned out to be possible to give quantum theory a closed mathematical formulation, essentially in terms of linear operators, acting on something which can in general be viewed as a space of multidimensional vectors, the "state vectors".

[vector: a set of numbers $A = (A_1,....,A_N)$, A_i: component. Vectors are added by adding their components. For linear operators e.g. $\mathbf{L} : \mathbf{L}(\alpha A+\beta B) = \alpha \mathbf{L}A+\beta \mathbf{L}B= \mathbf{L}(\alpha A_1,..) + \mathbf{L}(\beta B_1,..)$. In the ordinary two- or three-dimensional space, N=2,3 a vector can be pictured as an arrow. If $B_i = \gamma A_i$ *for all i*, B is parallel to A ; if $B_1A_1 + B_2A_2 + ... = 0$, B is perpendicular to A].

The connection to experiments is now given by the squares of "length" of these vector components (which are related to the length of the vector by a generalized pythagorean theorem , but in quantum mechanics usually $N > 3$, *even often infinite) giving probabilities* of results of certain measurements (one for each i). Probabilities are always positive, so it is natural that they are given by the *squares* of some numbers.

[In quantum mechanics, the A_is are often complex numbers, it is then the absolute square, also positive, which is used. The "wave functions" of quantum mechanics may be thought of as special vectors, where the index i is replaced by a continuous variable, say x, e.g. $A(x) = A_x$ (and A often replaced by a greek letter)].

The mathematical formalism tells us, e.g., how the *A's* develop in time. The consistency of this formalism is fairly obvious. The discussions between Bohr and Einstein were, however, rather concerned with the connection to experiment. Let *A* be a given vector with "length" unity. Now the length of a component is maximally one, corresponding to the probability of the corresponding measurement being smaller or equal to 100%. But if we look at two *different* components their lengths will in general both be smaller than unity corresponding to both results of measurements being only probable, not certain.

This is similar to ordinary statistics; when we measure properties of a physical system we are in general able to ascertain our measurements, so that some results become, say 99.9% probable, all other, say 0.1%, i.e. very improbable. What is peculiar to quantum mechanics is two features, directly seen from the vector picture. First we see that two state vectors, each representing a finite probability of a measurement, may add up – in quantum mechanical language producing a superposition of the states – to one state vector which corresponds to a probability which is far from the sum of the two probabilities, may be even zero, since it is the square of the vector's lengths which gives the probability.

Secondly, we see that if measurements of different quantities are *certain* for vectors in different *directions* then certainty of one result may *exclude* certainty in measurement of the other quantity. This will in the picture happen if the directions are skew (not perpendicular or parallel) to each other. The relation between such mutually exclusive measurements was by Bohr called complementarity. It is this feature which by *necessity* leads to a statistical description which has worried many physicists and philosophers, whereas the first feature, the superposition principle, gives rise to a number of spectacular phenomena which clearly show the simplicity and peculiarity of quantum mechanics, compared to classical mechanics. As the vector representation shows, the two features are intimately connected.

They are also connected to the fact, that all *measurements* are essentially classical, in the simple meaning that a single measurement always tells us whether – within given uncertainties – the measured variable *has* a given value or *not*. This may seem a truism, but is nevertheless the source of endless discussions about relations between language and facts. At the same time this measurement may imply that the state is a superposition of states corresponding to different values of *another* variable. If *this* is then measured, it will again have *one* of the values, so we see, that without the interpretation in terms of probabilities, the superposition has no clear meaning. Conversely, without the superposition, the probabilities would be just a particular case of classical probabilities. The connection between probability and absolute square of the vector length is sometimes called the Copenhagen interpretation, a terminology Bohr didn't like since – as I hope to have made plausible – there is no room for other physical interpretations of such a vector formalism.

It is of course *with* this interpretation rule, that quantum mechanics was shown to be a consistent *physical* theory.

For a long while Einstein did not feel satisfied. Probabilities, he argued, are known in many branches of physics, but generally they mean that we, due to insufficient data or insufficient theoretical methods – think of the weather forecasts – are unable to make precise predictions. Progress in science consists in overcoming such obstacles. In quantum mechanics where the precise knowledge of one variable may exclude precise knowledge of another, the statistics play another role and one might see this as a denial of the possibility of further progress. Einstein therefore suggested a number of thought experiments to see whether this exclusion of exact knowledge really could not, in principle, be overcome in some subtle way. Each time Bohr showed that although the experimental equipment must (in accordance with what was said above, about measurements being classical) be described classically, nevertheless some rudimentary aspects of quantum mechanics had to be included in terms of otherwise negligible uncertainties in determination of some parameters of this equipment. And when this was taken into account, the measurement possibilities corresponded exactly to the definition possibilities so that mutually excluding precisions in the formalism corresponded to mutually excluding, complementary, arrangements of equipment.

It is worth noting, that although many of these thought experiments have now been carried out in practice, and shown to be in complete agreement with quantum mechanics, this was not their historical role. *That* was not concerned with the *truth* of quantum mechanics, but with its *consistency*, somehow as a bad drawing on a blackboard may elucidate, e.g. whether a triangle can be constructed in agreement with the Euclidian geometry. One may also make triangularization experiments to investigate whether the *physical space* is *Euclidian*, but that is a completely different problem.

In the literature on the statistical aspects of quantum mechanics one often meets the notion of hidden variables. This refers to what we were saying above about statistics in other branches of physics often being forced upon us by an insufficient knowledge of the system. The superposition principle shows, however, that if the statistical spread of quantum results should be "explained" in terms of insufficient knowledge of "hidden" variables, these variables must have quite exceptional features which would e.g. exclude that a description where they *were* taken into account could be causal. Something similar is actually seen with the phenomena which we shall discuss next.

Another expression which is often met is that of the "collapse" of the wave function. This word may give the impression of some physical process but it refers actually to the above mentioned "truism" that a measurement always means that we go from a probability distribution to a definite result. Such a transition is of course inherent in the very definition of concepts like "probability distribution", "expectation value" etc. – think again of the weather forecasts or horse-race odds.

II. *Einstein, Podolsky and Rosen*

In the end Einstein accepted Bohr's proofs of consistency. It seems, nevertheless, that his feeling of dissatisfaction with quantum mechanics survived, and he raised new objections, which somehow are the roots of our present subject.

It also seems, that Einstein's accept was partly built on a misinterpretation of Bohr's arguments in the previous discussion. It is difficult to understand his new objections without thinking that Einstein must have thought that Bohr said that the lack of precision in determination of certain observables was *caused* by the measurement, e.g. by the light we used to look at the objects. There was for Bohr no question of such a causation which naturally could not even be *described* within the given framework of interplaying quantum mechanical and classical concepts. Bohr was concerned with the agreement between theoretical – in the sense of what the formalism gives – and experimental – in the sense of the *thought* experiments – possibilities of precise determination of observables.

Einstein's new objections have to do with systems composed of two parts. If the total system initially is in a definite state, a measurement of some property of one of the parts may, due to general conservation laws, determine a corresponding property of the other part without directly interacting with that.

As an example, a system with internal angular momentum (spin) 0 may decay into two parts, say each with angular momentum (spin) I. Now the angular momentum is classically a (n ordinary 3-dimensional) vector and the requirement that the total value is 0 will classically be fulfilled by the two vectors having opposite directions, in which case the measurement of one of them determines the direction of the other one.

In quantum mechanics the situation is both different and similar.

Thinking of one of the I-vectors, which classically has 3 components, say I_x, I_y, I_z the quantum mechanical formalism allows us to assign a precise value to *one* of these components only, excluding at the same time precise values of the two others. This "uncertainty" which distinguishes quantum mechanics from the classical can be correlated with the corresponding measurement possibilities with the usual arguments of Bohr. Note that we have freedom – related to the choice of experimental equipment – to choose *which* of the three components, more generally to which direction in space, a precise spin value is assigned.

What does *not* distinguish quantum mechanics from the classical is that once a component of one of the I's is determined, the *corresponding* component of the other is also given precisely, having the opposite value. This follows from the law of conservation of spin. From the same law, which is valid in quantum mechanics, as well as classical, it follows that the uncertainty of the values of the other components of the first I must give a corresponding uncertainty in determination of the other. If we think in terms of the above mentioned misinterpretation of Bohr's arguments, this becomes a riddle, when we are not interacting with this second part of our system. The two parts may in the meantime have moved to different places, so that no question of such an interaction may be raised.

Thus the prediction of quantum mechanics is that once the spin of the first part is measured along a certain direction, the probability of finding the spin of the second part in the opposite direction is 100 pct.If we measure it along another direction (still in the state with total spin 0) the probability is smaller. *After such* a measurement we have a new situation: The correlations corresponding to total spin 0, are destroyed – *this* destruction we can ascribe to the interaction in the measurement! – and the total spin has a finite probability of being different from 0). The whole story is actually similar to the case of only one part. We may determine one of its spin components, then we have a probability distribution for other spin components, which we may then measure, thus giving a probability prediction for the possible next measurement, and so forth.

Having the above description of the two part experiment in mind, the reader may find it difficult to understand Einstein's objections which were published in 1935 in an article with Podolsky and Rosen (*Physical Review*) (In this article, it is not spin components, but other mutually incompatible variables which are discussed, but the main issue is the same).

That these objections have nevertheless called for a world wide attention may partly be explained by Einstein's authority – he was after all not only the founder of the theory of relativity but also one of the founders of quantum mechanics. Partly the survival of the objections up to the 1980's may be due to their formulation in a somewhat obscure terminology.

EPR claim that quantum mechanics must be "incomplete" because it is in conflict with the following definition: "If, without in any way disturbing a system we can predict with certainty (i.e. with probability equal to unity) the value of a physical quantity, then there exists an element of physical reality corresponding to this physical quantity".

If we take our above example with spin components, the "element of physical reality" is, e.g., the I_z of the second system, when I_z of the first is measured. But let our apparatus be so that it measures I_x of the second system, then its I_z is uncertain and quantum mechanics describes the system as being in a superposition of states with different I_z values. Note, that the words first and second do not refer to a particular time sequence of the measurements, actually nothing in the experiment depends on this sequence.

The "consistency" in the first Bohr-Einstein discussion is more or less the usual consistency of logical-mathematical systems of concepts. The word "completeness" is used in a more special way. Incompleteness would usually mean that we could form statements within the formalism, the truth, or falseness,of which could not be decided in the formalism. Taking the statistical interpretation into account no such incompleteness has been seen.

The incompleteness of EPR is connected to the concept of "physical reality". It seems that EPR want to say that although I_z of the second part in the above experiment could only have a statistical distribution, it nevertheless in some way has a definite value, determined by the I_z measurement of the first part. It seems difficult to justify such a use of the words "element of physical reality". If we in stead say that the physical reality consists of the *measured* spin-components, we know that these in general permit only statistical predictions about the components of the other part of the system. But we also know that we get no contradictions, the statistical correlation being actually symmetric between the two systems. In the consistency discussion the point was, that it was not possible by subtle experimental arrangements to determine the value of observables with more certainty than the formalism allowed. In the present case we have of course the same if we want to use one part of the two part system to get knowledge of the other. This is recognized by EPR, but it seems that they nevertheless assume that in some abstract way this more precise knowledge exists as an element of physical reality.

That such a manner of speaking leads them to call quantum mechanics incomplete is in itself problematic. The most obvious objection against this use of the word "reality" is , however, connected with the superposition of states, as hinted in the first section.

Where is the "element of physical reality", if we in an experiment, from a superposition of two states which each has a finite probability of a certain result (say, a particle having a definite spin value or position) get one with zero probability?

One may perhaps conclude that even when speaking of "reality" one must be aware of the conditions for the use of such words.

Note, that it is the experimental arrangement which, as emphasized by Bohr, determines which quantities can be measured with certainty, not, as sometimes claimed, the observer (only as far as he determines which equipment to use). There is therefore no question about quantum mechanics giving up "realism" in favour of some "subjectivism".

(Note also that one of the philosophers who seems to have studied Bohr most carefully, Folse, classifies him as "realist") (2,3,4).

III. *Bohm, Aharonov and Bell*

The EPR article was answered, also in *Physical Review*, by Bohr, who mainly pointed out, how similar the suggested experiment really was to the thought experiments of their earlier discussions.

The "first" part of the system on which the measurement is performed corresponds to a part of the measuring apparatus. That this part in EPR is described quantum mechanically, whereas the apparatus is mainly described in classical terms is of no consequence. We are only talking of this part as having some well defined properties, i.e. we are talking classically, not in terms of superpositions of its states.

Although Bohr does not say so, we get the impression that he feels that Einstein had not quite appreciated his arguments of their earlier discussion. One also gets the impression, that already before the EPR paper, Einstein had ceased to have a genuine interest in quantum mechanics. He was working mainly with his theory of general relativity, and EPR has more the character of a play with concepts than of a contribution to physics. These and the following years were full of such contributions concerning, e.g.,the difficult task of reconciliating quantum mechanics with (Einstein's) theory of relativity. Much progress was achieved in this direction – though nothing that could shake the basis of Bohr's argumentation – but Einstein never later contributed to the development of quantum mechanics or to the investigation of its foundations.

In these years – i.e. from 1935 till now – some physicists and philosophers have from time to time been expressing uneasiness about quantum mechanics in general and about the so-called EPR paradox in particular.

Apart from Einstein's authority, the main reason is perhaps, that it *is* difficult to understand that the world can be like what quantum mechanics tells us, particularly if you are well adapted to the way of thinking of classical physics. If we particularly think of EPR where the determination of a variable (say a spin component) of one part leads to indeterminacy of another variable of another part (may be miles away), one may ask a number of questions. Could this be used to induce spin, e.g.,(and thereby transfer energy) over large distances in an immaterial way? The answer is of course no, since we have used conservation laws in deducing the effect.

Or could it be used to transmit information with a speed higher than light? Again no, the indeterminacy does not contain information.

For non-physicists it may throw some light on these extraordinary features of quantum physics when you imagine similar situations to occur in ordinary life. Think of a dialogue:

A: Did you vote yes or no in the referendum?

B: It is of no consequence; C and I had agreed in the morning that it is bad for democracy not to vote, but, since none of us had any opinion about the issue, we should take opposite standpoints – so our votes have annihilated each other!
A: But you must after all have decided whether to vote yes or no. How?
B: Oh, I just made the cross with closed eyes!
A: But how could you then tell C how to vote? She was in another voting box at the same time!
B: But I just told you that we had agreed how to vote already in the morning!
A: ?!!??!

Like the other thought experiments the EPR idea was mainly meant to expose quantum mechanics, to show how "strange" its consequences were, whereas the tests whether it was correct were contained in the general application of quantum mechanics to physical phenomena. It has in this respect been extremely successful, explaining, e.g., all stability properties of matter (classical mechanics has no room for real stability). If those who felt uneasy about quantum mechanics had hoped that it were refuted, they were disappointed (uneasiness about classical physics would have been more appropriate). That was perhaps the reason why some physicists turned to the thought experiments in the opinion that these were crucial experiments for quantum mechanics, which had, however, never been performed.

Although by far the main stream in physics is still the quest for new phenomena, new particles etc., a number of, say, more scholarly oriented experimentalists are in the later years actually concentrating their efforts on carrying such "thought experiments" out in practice. They have here e.g. used the improved possibilities of controlling the temperature of the apparatus very precisely. In the old days it was often argued, that heat fluctuations would in practice wipe out many of the typical quantum effects, discussed in the thought experiments. Recently these and many other problems were overcome, and most of the thought experiments of the old discussions (as well as many similar, which were *not* discussed at that time) *have* been *made* and within the still existing error limits have given results in agreement with quantum mechanics.

Among these, the two-part experiments of EPR type have been some of the more difficult to carry out in practice. This is presumably mainly due to the requirement that the two parts should be observed when they were so far apart that there really was no question of interacting with one when observing the other. At the same time the correlations must not be wiped out. If we e.g. think of the two opposite spins mentioned above, any small fluctuations of a field which could make the spins turn, will in general have larger effects the longer time the systems with the spin are moving in the field. So we see, that the two requirements may be difficult to fulfil in one experiment. Similar difficulties are seen with other variables.

Spin and related variables came into prominence because the correlations may lead to predictions of experimental results formulated in particularly simple mathematical terms. It was Bohm and Aharonov who already in 1957 suggested to use spins. For this case the late John Bell gave a simple mathematical formulation of the difference between a quantum mechanical description, where correlations and statistical fluctuations somehow go together, and a classical description, where statistical fluctuations are only possible in connection with destruction of correlations. We shall below look at a slightly modified – by Clauser, Horne and Shimony – version of what is called Bell's inequalities.

The point is that we will instead of spin – a variable which is anyhow not very familiar to non-physicists – think of *polarized light* (used in cameras, sunglasses etc.).

This is a well known *classical* phenomenon: light is electromagnetic oscillations, where the electric (and the magnetic) field vector is always perpendicular to the direction of propagation of the light.

This requirement still gives a continuum of possible directions of the field, and ordinary light contains a mixture of such directions.

In *polarized* light, the electric field is oscillating in *one* direction. Classically, this means that if one asks for the field in another direction, one has a force component, corresponding to the projection of the field on this other direction. If particularly it is *perpendicular* to the field, the component has magnitude zero. Note, that since the field is oscillating, *opposite* directions are equivalent.

In quantum mechanics, light is, however occurring in finite portions – "photons". We then have, when photon numbers are small, again a *probabilistic* description. Instead of measuring a stronger or weaker field component, one either measures one photon or none, but the theory gives a continuously varying *probability* for such a measurement.

It is typical that to classically measurable properties correspond similar, precisely measurable quantities in quantum mechanics, with corresponding states which however – as mentioned above – do not allow for a simultaneous precise definition of certain *other* properties.

Here the polarisation along a certain direction is such a property. As in the classical case the opposite direction represents the *same* polarisation. A 100% polarisation along these directions mean *no* polarisation along a direction perpendicular to these (and to the light direction). So this is then *also* precisely given, in quantum as well as in classical mechanics. What will *not* have a precise meaning is the polarisation in a skew direction, say 45° with respect to the measured polarisation direction (still perpendicular to the light propagation). Technically the polarisation measurement is, in agreement with what we said about its relation to the classical one, made with a "filter", the analyzer, which permits 100% penetration of light polarized in a definite direction (0% perpendicular to that), and behind that a detector, which registers one or zero photons (5,6,7).

IV. *The Aspect Experiment*

In this experiment we look at an atom which is in a state of total angular momentum – "spin" – 0 and which decays by successively emitting two photons to end up in a state of spin 0.

The two photons have obviously together carried no angular momentum away from the system. Each of the photons carries one unit of internal angular momentum, spin, so the two spins are obviously correlated. Now the spin and polarisation of photons are actually intimately related, so also the two polarisations are correlated. Let the two photons propagate in opposite directions along an axis, which we may use as Z-axis in an ordinary rectangular coordinate system. Then the correlation means, that we have a total wave function which is a *sum* of two components, one where both photons are polarized in the X-direction, one where they are both polarized in the Y-direction (X and Y mean any two directions which are mutually orthogonal and orthogonal to the propagation direction (Z)). So we have here again a situation similar to that of the spins: If we e.g. measure the polarisation of one photon to be along the x-axis we immediately can predict that *if* we measure the polarisation of the other photon along the same axis, it is 100% sure to have that polarisation. But this does not mean that it always *has* such a polarisation, if we measure along the y-axis we would get analogous results:

the *correlation* is 100% but the polarisation itself is (completely) indeterminate; the chances that both photons are X-polarised is the same as the chance that both are Y-polarised: 50%.

A little less trivial is the case where we measure one photon polarisation along the X direction and another along another, "skew" direction, X_1 say with an angle v to the X. The probability is now proportional to he square of the coefficient that represents the projection of one state vector on the other: $R = 0.5cos^2v$, which actually gives us back ½ when the two directions are parallel.

This is a *particularly simple* case, where the state vectors can be pictured as ordinary vectors in ordinary space. (In general the state vectors of a system may have many dimensions. Then the length of their projections on each other, the square of which represent the corresponding probabilities of finding a system simultaneously in the two corresponding states, will depend on many parameters, not only one angle).

If we ask about the probability of finding the polarisation of the second photon along the second direction, *without* measuring the polarisation of the first, we find actually that it is again ½, a very plausible result.

Let us now for a moment forget about these quantum mechanical facts and try a description of our two-photon experiments in terms of ordinary statistical theories. Let us call the probability that we measure one photon polarised along the X direction, the other along the X_1 direction $P(X_1,X_2^1)$ and the probability that we measure one photon along the X direction without measuring the other $P(X_1)$. Here $0 \leqslant P(X_1) \leqslant 1$ etc.

Suppose now, as hinted earlier, that the statistical description is related to our lack of knowledge of some variables, the "Hidden Parameters" , which we shall together call q. Then the possibilities must somehow depend on those q values:

$$P(X) = P(q;X);\ P(X_1,X_2^1) = P(q;X_1,X_2^1)$$

etc. But, and this is a crucial point, if the theory is sufficiently normal (if e.g. the hidden variables interact with the observed ones locally, so that the events in the two ends of the experiment don't influence each other), we must have

$$P(q;\ X_1,X_2^1) = P(q;\ X_1)\ P(q;X_2^1)$$

(Note that in this experiment the two photons are distinguishable, being measured at different detectors (and having different energies)).

Now we look at a series of experiments where the two photons are analyzed (:their polarization is measured) in one of two directions for each:

$$[X_1,X_2^1],[X_2,X_2^1]$$

Now

$$0 \leqslant P(X_1^1)(1 - P(X_2^1)) + P(X_2)(1 - P(X_1^1)) + P(X_1)(P(X_2^1) - P(X_2)) \leqslant 1$$

or

$$0 \leqslant P(X_1)P(X_2^1)+P(X_1^1)+P(X_2)-P(X_1)P(X_2)-P(X_1^1)P(X_2)-P(X_1^1)P(X_2^1) \leqslant 1$$

According to the usual interpretation of probabilistic predictions (the law of big numbers) we have that for a sufficiently long series of measurements the number of photons polarized along a certain axis, say X_1, relative to the total number must be

$$S(X_1) = N(X_1)/N = \int dqW(q)\ P(q;X_1)$$

etc. where W(q) is a function which weights the different q values in the average according to some underlying theory.

We then also have

$$0 \leqslant S(X_1^1,X_2^1) + S(X^1) + S(X_2) - S(X_1,X_2) - S(X_1^1,X_2) - S(X_1^1,X_2^1)$$

The same inequality must of course be valid if we in stead of S write $R = S/S_0$, where S_0 is the ratio counted without analyzing the polarisations, keeping only the photon counters.

We have seen, however, that according to quantum mechanics, the corresponding number is

$$R(X_1,X_2^1) = 0.5cos^2v(X_1,X_2^1)$$

We now choose

$$\nu(X_1,X_2) = \nu(X_2^1,X_1^1) = \nu(X_2,X_1^1) = \pi : 8 = 22.5^0$$

(so $\nu(X_1,X_2^1) = 67.5^0$,the reader may try to draw the X-vectors as an illustration, also the (Bell) inequalities may be illustrated by picturing the products as areas). Now

$$R(X_1^1) + R(X_2) + R(X_1,X_2^1) - R(X_1,X_2^1) - R(X_1^1,X_2^1) - R(X_1^1,X_2)$$

$$= 0.5 + 0.5 + 0.25 - 0.75 - 0.25(3+1)\sqrt{2}0.5 = 0.5(1 - \sqrt{2}) < 0$$

This is an example of the statement that quantum mechanics is in disagreement with inequalities of the Bell's type. Actually the result as given above is founded on assuming the analyzers and detectors to work in an ideal way. However, the deviations from these ideal cases are *known* and can be taken into account. When this is done the above number may, for the famous Aspect experiment, be estimated to be -0.1 instead of $0.5(1- \sqrt{2}) \sim -0.2$, and this is also what was found experimentally.

There have actually been made a number of experiments which in this way prove the superiority of quantum mechanics relative to theories with hidden variables. There were, however, raised a number of objections against most of these experiments. The objection which, strange to say, has been taken most seriously is that it could be difficult to exclude completely that the polarization measurement of one photon was influenced by the position of the other analyzer.

The achievement of Aspect must be seen in this context. He constructed an ingenious apparatus which could switch from X_1 to X_1^1 in a hundredth of a millionth of a second, and similarly with X_2,X_2^1 (using light scattering on standing sound waves for the analyzers). The lifetime of the intermediate (spin 1) state between the two photo emissions is half as long, and the time it takes for the light to go from the source to the analyzers-detectors is four times the switching time. According to the (generally accepted) theory of relativity no signal can travel faster than light, so it is absolutely excluded that any message can reach from the analyzer-detector of one photon to those of the other,in order to influence the measurement.

It would of course be best if we were ourselves choosing whether X_1 or X_1^1

should be measured. Thinking of human reaction times this would have required enormously much larger dimensions of the experimental arrangement, thus again introducing difficulties mentioned above. Aspects idea was to let the *apparatus* chose in such a way that it would be practically impossible for any mechanism with hidden parameters to fake the quantum mechanical results.

The experiment completely confirmed the expectations from quantum mechanics.

Rumours has it, that Bell was then inclined to convert to a "holistic" interpretation of quantum mechanics, perhaps along similar lines as have been suggested by David Bohm. Note, though, that correlations are only seen between photons emitted from the same atom, i.e. causally connected!

Quite a number of physicists received the news about Aspect's experiment very calmly. First of all, of course, because it was a confirmation of a hypothesis they had already accepted: Quantum mechanics as such had already long before ceased to be a field of front research; it had become a tool which was used every day by theoreticians and experimentalists. Using this tool, even in the same years, very strange new experimental and theoretical discoveries were made. It was e.g. found that a number of hitherto accepted elementary particles were composed of some more fundamental building stones, the quarks, but that these quarks could never be observed as isolated entities.

We have further seen that the result of Aspect's admirable experiment may be formulated that one photon measurement could not be influenced by the other, because the message would have to travel faster than light. This formulation also gives a clue to understanding the calmness with which the news were received by many physicists.

The point is that, even without thinking of the light velocity, the whole idea of such a message is rather absurd. There is nothing in the experimental circumstances, which are after all simple, that gives the slightest hint of what could be the nature of such a signal, carrying a complicated information about macroscopic states of the apparatus. This is in sharp contrast to usual arguments in physics, where signals are connected to well defined phenomena as motions of masses or charges etc.

It should also be noted that although the two photons clearly are coming in a definite time sequence, their roles in the experiment are again completely parallel. So we see that even disregarding the requirements of the theory of relativity, we may think of the hypothetical signals as going backwards as well as forwards in time.

All together the discussion related to Bell's inequalities and Aspect's experiments reminds more of, say, the logical deductions which in a novel permits the detective to exclude one suspect after the other, than of the mixture of conservatism and radicalism, of mathematics, common sense and philosophical speculations, which usually characterizes scientific thinking (8,9).

Literature

1. N. Bohr, "Discussions with Einstein", in Schilpp (ed.) *Albert Einstein: Philosopher – Scientist*, Evanstone, Library of Living Philosophers, 1949, p. 202.
2. A. Einstein, B. Podolsky, and N. Rosen, "Can Quantum-Mechanical Description of Physical Reality be Considered Complete?", *Physical Review* **47**, 777 (1935).
3. N. Bohr, "Can Quantum-Mechanical description of Physical Reality be Considered Complete?" *Physical Review* **48**, 696 (1935).
4. H. J. Folse, *The Philosophy of Niels Bohr*, North-Holland, Amsterdam, 1985.
5. D. Bohm and Y. Aharonov, "Discussions of Experimental Proof for the Paradox of Einstein, Rosen and Podolsky" *Physical Review* **108**, 1070 (1957).
6. J. S. Bell, *Physics* **1**, 195 (1965).
7. J. F. Clauser and A. Shimony, "Bell's Theorem: Experimental Tests and Implications", *Rep.Prog.Phys.* **41**, 1881 (1978).
8. A. Aspect, J. Dalibard, and G. Roger, "Experimental Test of Bell's Inequalities Using Time-Varying Analyses", *Physical Review Letters* **49**, 1804 (1982).
9. J. Bang and B. Lautrup, "David Bohms Virkelighed", *Omverden*, nr. 3 (1990). (in danish, an english translation can be obtained).

Danish Yearbook of Philosophy, Vol. **27** (1992), 109-118

BOHR'S QUANTUM PHILOSOPHY: ON THE SHOULDER OF A GIANT?

HELGE KRAGH
Roskilde University Centre

Review of:
Jan Faye, *Niels Bohr: His Heritage and Legacy* (Dordrecht: Kluwer Academic Publishers, 1991), 263 pages.

It is the fate, and sometimes misfortune, of great scientists to be scrutinized by historians and philosophers of science aiming at establishing what external influences determined their thoughts and actions. The question of how and why a creative individual – whether a scientist, philosopher or artist – arrived at a particular view is not only legitimate to ask and attempt to answer; it is central to the historian who seeks explanation and not mere description in the history of ideas. As one of the greatest scientists ever, Niels Bohr has often been the subject of such attempts at explanation, although in his case the attempts have not so much been directed towards his purely scientific works as towards his philosophical interpretation of quantum physics and views on its wider consequences. Few people have dared to "explain" the emergence of Bohr's 1913 atomic theory in terms of cultural influences, but many have offered such explanations with respect to Bohr's correspondence and complementarity principles and the Copenhagen interpretation of quantum physics in general. A common feature in most of these attempts is that the explanans is a philosopher or philosophical school, and that Bohr's views are seen as explained if they can be traced back to the influence of a philosopher (somehow the philosopher's view does not seem to be in need of similar explanation). With more or less luck, mostly less, in ny opinion, Bohr's views have been traced back to influences of William James, Harald Høffding or Søren Kierkegaard. Less serious candidates for spiritual paternity have been Ernst Mach, Edgar Rubin and – of course! – Immanuel Kant.

Jan Faye believes to have succeeded where others have failed, and to have shown that "Høffding was Bohr's intellectual father and mentor." This is the central thesis of the book, issued as volume 6 in Kluwer's series *Science and Philosophy*. The paternity claim should be understood in the sense that (1) Høffding exerted a direct and crucial philosophical influence on Bohr; (2) this influence shaped Bohr's philosophical thinking on quantum physics to the extent that (3) had it not been for Høffding, Bohr would not have formulated the complementarity principle and his anti-realism in the way he did. I shall refer to this claim as the Høffding thesis. Whereas this is a historical claim which is argued historically, the book also contains an analytic-philosophical part in which Faye examines Bohr's quantum philosophy in the light of his thesis that this philosophy was inherited from Høffding. More about this below.

II

The problem of the ontological status of quantum mechanics in Bohr's philosophy and the associated Copenhagen interpretation belongs to the most discussed subjects of modern philosophy of science. According to one common view, Bohr was an anti- or at least non-realist in the sense that he denied the wave function an ontological status and furthermore held an epistemic notion of truth, i.e., that truth clams must relate to forms of cognition which are not determined by the objective world. Bohr denied that transphenomenal objects can be ascribed reality and often defended the instrumentalist-sounding claim that the goal of physics is not the understanding of nature but the realization of unambiguous communication about experience. In spite of this, several Bohr scholars have concluded that Bohr was, after all, a realist of some sort. Henry Folse, in particular, has argued that Bohr's philosophy is incompatible with phenomenalism and includes a belief in ontologically independent microphysical objects.[1] In this sense Bohr's philosophy is claimed to be a brand of realism. Faye disagrees.

Faye's book offers an interesting and penetrating analysis of the problem of realism in Bohr's thinking. According to this analysis, Bohr was indeed not a phenomenalist in the Machian sense, which does not, however, mean that he was therefore a realist. Since Bohr, in Faye's view, considered truth a feature of our cognitive faculties and rejected the idea of sub- or transphenomenal objects, he was an anti-realist all the same. Faye arrives at this view in the same way as Folse arrives at his, namely by philosophical analysis, that is, by examination of the relationship of between Bohrian complementarity and the notions of realism and anti-realism, respectively. But Faye goes beyond merely labelling Bohr's position as anti-realism, which concept he qualifies in an interesting and original way. In opposition to the radically anti-realistic and anti-ontological view argued especially by Aage Petersen[2] – "ontological nihilism" as Faye aptly names the position – he argues that quantum mechanics is not devoid of ontological commitments, only they refer to experimental conditions ("phenomena") rather than objects. Bohr's view can thus be accommodated with the notion of atomic objects being real without leading to realism if only it is accepted that the modes of existence of the atomic objects depend on mental faculties.

This idea corresponds to Faye's distinction, inspired by Michael Dummett, between to kinds of anti-realism, an objective and a subjective one. The latter version holds that the external world is mind-dependent, and thus leads to idealism. Bohr was clearly not an idealist. Objective anti-realism, on the other hand, shares with the subjective version the belief in truth depending on or relating to mental faculties, but it combines this anti-realist feature with the belief in an objective world that exists independent of our mind. Faye shows the consistency of such a position and emphasizes that notions of objectivity are not necessarily incompatible with anti-realism. It will now be clear that Faye's position with regard to Bohr's thinking can be summarized in the statement that the Danish quantum sage was an objective anti-realist.

But what has all this to do with Høffding? Quite a lot, according to Faye, who claims that Bohr inherited his anti-realism from the old philosopher. Now Høffding regarded himself a realist and would probably have been surprised to find himself being placed in the anti-realist camp. However, a closer reading of Høffding's works – Faye's closer reading – reveals that he was in fact an objective anti-realist, and Faye can thus contend that Bohr received his view on microphysical reality through Høffding. The documentary evidence for this particular claim of influence is weak, though. The claim rests essentially on analytical comparison between Bohr's and Høffding's writings, or rather on comparison between philosophical reconstructions of these writings. For in this case also Høffding has to be interpreted constructively in order to make him an objective anti-realist.

As I see it, the value of Faye's discussion of realism in quantum physics is independent of the associated historical claim, the Høffding thesis. Whether or not Høffding influenced Bohr in this respect is of marginal philosophical interest, whereas the interpretation of Bohr as an objective anti-realist is in itself philosophically interesting. It is possible that the claimed Høffding link leads to a better understanding also of Høffding's philosophy, but not being a Høffding scholar I shall leave this topic alone. The Høffding thesis may be looked upon heuristically, as a tool by means of which new and possibly fruitful aspects of the philosophies of Høffding and, in particular, Bohr are obtained. However, this is not the way Jan Faye looks upon it. To him the historical connection is an integral part of the correct philosophical understanding, and his aim is a much historical as it is philosophical.

III

The idea that Høffding played a major role in shaping Bohr's thinking was suggested many years ago by Max Jammer and has since then appeared regularly. But it is only with Faye's work that the idea has been argued in an elaborated and tightly knit manner which deserves serious attention. As far as the Høffding thesis is concerned, Faye's book rests heavily on a couple of earlier papers, which are here supplied with further historical evidence and presented in a coherent way.[3] Faye's thesis has developed alongside with and partly in opposition to a series of papers by David Favrholdt, who since 1976 has argued against the attempts to place Bohr's thoughts on the shoulders of philosophers, giants or not.[4] Favrholdt's criticism is not exclusively directed against the Høffding thesis, but also against the corresponding Kierkegaard and James theses (or "myths," in Favrholdt's terminology). As far as these are concerned, Faye's answer is clear: To the extent that James and Kierkegaard influenced Bohr at all, they did so through Høffding who acted not only as an inspiration in his own right but also as a prism through which other philosophical views were filtered before they reached the mind of the young Bohr.

In this context I would like to point out the danger of judging by implication, for example by associating Faye's work with earlier and easily criticizable attempts to link Bohr's views with Kierkegaard. Lewis Feuer made such an attempt in 1974, where he without further argumentation "explained" Bohr's 1913 notion of quantum jumps as a kind of subconscious reworking of Kierkegaard's idea of "leaps" during an individual's life.[5] Although Faye's project may be said to belong to the same broad category of cultural externalism, it differs fundamentally from Feuers' both in its emphasis on Høffding (and not Kierkegaard) and, particularly, in its documentation and level of argumentation. To discuss Faye's scholarly and well-argued Høffding thesis as merely another version of Feuer's claim would not be fair. Neither is it reasonable to term Faye's version of the Høffding thesis a "myth, for it does not seem to have the social and legitimizing functions that characterize myths. It may be wrong, as I think it is, but it is not a myth.

Incidentally, Faye's book contains an in-depth and lucid examination of Høffding's philosophy of science, which, irrespective of the validity of the Høffding-Bohr claim, is of great interest. It may well be the most significant impact of the book that it re-introduces Høffding to an international public. Faye's picture of the great original thinker Høffding, who anticipated modern philosophy of science, may not be accepted, but there will be left a solid account of his accomplishments and perhaps a stimulus for further work. In this as in other respects Faye's zealous attempt to prove the Høffding thesis (and Favrholdt's to disprove it) have resulted in considerable historical insight, including the unearthing of new sources. These are of some value insofar as they illuminate details in Bohr's life, but Faye seems to exaggerate their scientific and philosophical importance.

IV

The question of an individual H influencing the thoughts of another individual B has to be qualified or broken down into several sub questions. These include: (1) In what areas did H influence B? (2) During which period? (3) To what extent? In the case examined by Faye the first question is answered by claiming that Høffding influenced Bohr's philosophical conception of physics and indeed his entire way of thinking about physical problems. The period of direct influence lasted from about 1903 to 1930, during which years Høffding deeply and decisively shaped Bohr's thoughts. These claims are not to be refuted off-hand, for in the history of ideas we know of influences of a similarly strong kind. As Faye mentions, nobody questions that Plato was deeply and decisively influenced by Socrates. The analogy is apt in more than one respect (but not in all), for in the background of the controversy over the Høffding thesis lurks the question of Bohr's greatness and originality as a philosopher. However, the possible deflation of Bohr as a philosophical thinker is in principle irrelevant for the evaluation of the Høffding claim. And, anyway, has the appreciation of Plato as one of the greatest philosophers ever suffered from the fact that he was influenced by Socrates?

On the other hand, one should be cautious to accept influence claims, if for no other reason then because historical scholarship in a number of cases has proved these to be exaggerated or unfounded. The Einstein-Mach case may be typical. As is well known, Einstein acknowledged on several occasions Mach's influence and it is fairly easy to establish epistemic similarities between the two thinkers. Yet Mach and Einstein scholars believe that although Mach did influence the great physicist in certain ways, the influence was neither decisive nor of the extent indicated by Einstein himself.

By and large, and wisely, Faye restricts his claim to the level of philosophy and refrains from saying that Bohr's heritage from Høffding had also a direct effect on his works in physics proper. But in Bohr's case it is difficult to separate sharply his philosophical views on and attitudes to physics from his scientific works, and at least implicitly Faye indicates that Høffding was also of crucial importance to Bohr's physical theories up to the early 1930s. Consider the correspondence principle, which was an integral element of Bohr's theories of multiply periodic systems and the structure of higher atoms in the period 1918-24 and which acted as much as a quantitative scientific method as a heuristic guide of a philosophical nature. Faye believes that the correspondence principle was indebted to Høffding at least in the sense that Bohr's understanding of its nature and implications was part of the Høffding heritage. Incidentally, he finds it "interesting" that the principle was originally (1918-20) known as a principle of analogy, for Høffding used the word "analogy" in a sense which, if a very charitable reading is adopted, can be related to Bohr's principle. This I find a rather far-fetched analogy (if the reader will excuse me). I see no reason to invoke Høffding in the genesis or application of the principle, whereas I find it less implausible that Høffding may have inspired Bohr's later interpretation of it. After all, the correspondence principle was a relatively straightforward generalization of the approach already taken in 1913, and the 1918 presentation depends on simple physical reasoning in no need of additional philosophical influence. Furthermore, in the years up to about 1927, when the correspondence principle ceased to play an important scientific role, it was used routinely as a tool by physicists, many of whom had no association with Bohr.

Even less acceptable is it when Faye claims that "when Bohr developed his [1913] theory of the structure of the hydrogen atom, it was on the basis of the methodological precept he had learned from Høffding." As far as I know, the genesis of Bohr's atomic theory has been satisfactorily accounted for without any reference at all to particular methodological precepts.[7] There is simply no need to consider philosophical influences in this case. I consider Faye's brief reference to the 1913 theory merely a minor blemish, though, for otherwise he is careful in distinguishing between science and philosophizing about science.

V

What kind of evidence are we looking for in order to establish an influence claim of the Høffding-Bohr type? In other words, what are the criteria for accepting that B was decisively influenced by H? This central question in the historiography of ideas is, at the same time, simple and frustratingly vexed. In some cases direct and unambiguous links may be established through, for example, the diaries and notebooks of B. This is the way the intellectual influences on Darwin have been ascertained, but unfortunately Bohr left us no sources of a corresponding authenticity and reliability. Faye realizes that the Høffding claim cannot be prove and that the entire claim has to be based on evaluation of documentary evidence combined with analytical thinking. To establish an influence claim, Faye says, it should satisfy the following two conditions: (1) There must be a causal connection from H to B, and (2) there must be an epistemic correspondence between the stated views of H and B. These are reasonable conditions, but in fact too stringent to count as necessary, for H may well influence B in the absence of any positive epistemic correspondence. Thus, Darwin undoubtedly influenced many non-evolutionists to argue the very opposite of his own ideas. The important thing is that confirmation of intellectual influence claims are always of an evidential nature. This is quite clear to Faye, who makes no secret of the fact that such claims rest "with Judgment" and that "Ultimately, it [the Høffding thesis] will depend on a personal assessment as to whether the evidence shows that the ideas are sufficiently similar and that the causal connection is sufficiently well-documented for us to conclude that a person acquired some of his ideas from another individual." With this recognition it is neither surprising nor objectionable that Faye's book is filled with phrases such as "I believe that", "it is reasonable to believe", and "I find the evidence sufficient to conclude". Although it makes strict objectivity impossible, this is the rule of the game, and one which is well-known to historians.

VI

But because of its circumstantial and non-objective nature reasoning from sources is a tricky matter which may play games even with experienced and critical historians. On the whole Faye handles the historical material (letters, manuscripts, published sources) admirably, but it is all too evident that he is "biased" in his wish to demonstrate the Høffding thesis (of course he is, and of course he should be!). Favrholdt has, not entirely without reasons, accused Faye of reading his preconceived ideas into the source material and of discovering influences and analogies where none are; on his side, Faye has accused Favrholdt of closing his eyes to the pro-Høffding thesis evidence, as were he another Nelson (or perhaps a pontifical scholar when confronted with Galileo's telescopic evidence). At any rate, Faye's documentary evidence is extensive and cleverly presented. He points out that Bohr attended Høffding's lectures in propaedeutic philosophy and argues that he also followed some of Høffding's more advanced seminars. Then there is the Ekliptika Circle – the discussion club of which Bohr was a member and which discussed Høffding's ideas – and the continuing close contact between Bohr and Høffding (whether this contact was really close and scientific has been questioned by Favrholdt). Finally Faye points out, quite correctly, that most likely his collected evidence systematically underestimates the contacts between Bohr and Høffding. Both sages lived in Copenhagen and, argues Faye, must have had numerous encounters of which we have no written evidence. This is undoubtedly true, but it is a fact which we can make no use of.

Sources should be read in their historical context, which implies bringing in background knowledge and using this for reading also between the lines. Faye does so, but tends to reserve his critical reading for cases which support his claim. The "historical context" seems to play a lesser role when it indicates a weakening of the Høffding thesis. One case in point is the social contexts in which several of Bohr's own references to Høffding appeared, namely celebratory or memorial events, such as the address Bohr gave to the Psychology Congress in 1932 shortly after Høffding's death. Texts are always directed at a public and will to a certain extent reflect the anticipations of that public or social norms in general. In other words, they cannot be taken at their face value. For example, in 1931 Einstein strongly indicated that Michelson's ether-drift experiments provided the starting point for his development of the theory of relativity, although we know that in fact this was not the case.[8] As Einstein's testimony can be understood if related to its social context – the speech was given at a meeting in honour of Michelson – so some of Bohr's testimonies should be read as tributes to Høffding rather than factual statements.

Belonging to a somewhat different category is the evaluation of "negative evidence," that is, the lack of statements of influence where one would expect such to turn up. When Høffding did not refer to discussions with Bohr in his memoirs of 1928 (*Erindringer*), what does it signify? Without going into the details of the Faye-Favrholdt dispute concerning this point, my impression is that Faye dismisses this kind of negative evidence too easily. There are a few other cases of questionable interpretation and too easy analogizing in Faye's book, but I see them as relatively innocent results of Faye's eagerness in supporting his claim. They do not materially alter the overall situation that there is evidence for the claim, but that the sources are ambiguous and do not lead to Faye's strong claim.

VII

In conclusion, Jan Faye has provided evidence for the connection between Høffding and Bohr and shown that some of Bohr's philosophical views may be interpreted as reflecting an influence either directly from Høffding or mediated through him. But he has not succeeded in building up a convincing case for the claim that Bohr was strongly or decisively influenced by Høffding, let alone that Høffding was the spiritual father of the complementarity philosophy. This conclusion is of course my personal judgment, based on critical reading of Faye's book and whatever subconscious biases I may have. As mentioned, there are no methods for deciding the matter objectively and hence I cannot pretend to have refuted the Høffding thesis, only to have argued its lack of solid foundation.

The historical problems apart, Faye has offered interesting and clever analyses of both Bohr's and Høffding's philosophies. He has done so informed by his wish to confirm the Høffding thesis, but the fact (that is, my conclusion) that he has failed to do so does not invalidate or render irrelevant the analytical parts of the book. My criticism notwithstanding, I find Faye's work interesting and valuable in its interpretation of Niels Bohr's quantum philosophy.

Notes

1. H. Folse, *The Philosophy of Niels Bohr: The Framework of Complementarity* (Amsterdam: North-Holland, 1985).
2. Aa. Petersen, *Quantum Physics and the Philosophical Tradition* (Cambridge, Mass.: MIT Press, 1968).
3. J. Faye, "The influence of Harald Høffding's philosophy on Niels Bohr's interpretation of quantum mechanics", *Danish Yearbook of Philosophy* 16 (1979), 37-72; "The Bohr-Høffding relationship reconsidered," *Studies in the History and Philosophy of Science* 19 (1988), 321-46.
4. D. Favrholdt, "Niels Bohr and Danish philosophy," *Danish Yearbook of Philosophy* 13 (1976), 206-20; "On Høffding and Bohr," *Ibid.* 16 (1979), 73-77; "The cultural background of the young Bohr," *Rivista di Storia della Scienza* 2 (1985), 445-61; "Remarks on the Bohr-Høffding relationship," *Studies in the History and Philosophy of Science* 22 (1991), 399-414; "Niels Bohr's philosophical background," *Kgl. Da. Vid. Selskab, Hist.-Fil. Meddelelser* 63 (1992), 1-147.
5. L. Feuer, *Einstein and the Generations of Science* (New York: Basic Books, 1974).
6. J. Blackmore, *Ernst Mach: A Deeper Look* (Dordrecht: Kluwer, 1992)
7. J. L. Heilbron and T. S. Kuhn, "The genesis of the Bohr atom," *Historical Studies in the Physical Sciences* 1 (1969), 211-90. U. Hoyer, *Die Geschichte der Bohrschen Atomtheorie* (Weinheim: Physik Verlag, 1974).
8. *Cf.* H. Kragh, *An Introduction to the Historiography of Science* (Cambridge: Cambridge University Press, 1987), p. 153.